101 BOUNCY BIBLE RHYME-TIME GAMES
for Children's Ministry

BY

DAWN M. BENEGAR

Group
Loveland, Colorado

101 Bouncy Bible Rhyme-Time Games for Children's Ministry

Copyright © 2000 Dawn M. Benegar

Visit our Web site: **www.grouppublishing.com**

CREDITS
Editor: Linda A. Anderson
Creative Development Editor: Jody Brolsma
Chief Creative Officer: Joani Schultz
Copy Editor: Betty Taylor
Art Director/Designer: Jean Bruns
Cover Art Director: Jeff A. Storm
Cover Designer: Liz Howe
Cover Illustrator: Kathy Couri
Computer Graphic Artist: Fred Schuth
Illustrators: Eulala Connor, Shelley Dieterichs, Kathie Kelleher
Production Manager: Peggy Naylor

Library of Congress Cataloging-in-Publication Data
ISBN 0-7644-2217-0

10 9 8 7 6 5 4 3 2 1   09 08 07 06 05 04 03 02 01 00

Printed in the United States of America.

CONTENTS

Jump-Rope Rhymes

Chinese Jump-Rope Rhymes

Hand Games

String Games

Ball Games

Hopscotch Games

Dedication

This book is wholly dedicated to God, because he gave us the ideas and the words to write. He brought people to encourage and cheer us. This book is here for you to enjoy solely because of his work in our lives. We pray that this book will be used to reach the hearts and minds of many people for his glory.

"Praise and glory
and wisdom and thanks and honor
and power and strength
be to our God for ever and ever.
Amen" (Revelation 7:12).

Acknowledgments

Brett Benegar, husband and dad, who helped and put up with me as I worked on this book.

Arlie Benegar, mother and grandmother, who has been supportive and has even written a couple of the rhymes.

Mary Lee Carl, a close friend, who gave many ideas and spent much time helping me put the ideas together.

Elaine Francis and her son Matthew, also friends, who contributed time and ideas. Elaine helped me correct the rhymes so that they flowed well. Matthew created some of the string shapes.

Debbie D. Johnson, another friend, who spent time helping refine the work and contributed a few rhymes.

Friends and neighbors who have supported me, encouraged me, and cheered me on as I wrote this book.

The Keenagers group of Washington Heights Baptist Church who willingly shared their experiences of playtime when they were young.

A special thanks to my editor, Linda A. Anderson, who was encouraging to a new writer on a compressed schedule.

I believe God brought all these people to help me for his glory and honor.

A special acknowledgment

My daughters, Jessica and Britni, were vital contributors to this book. Even though their names are not on the cover, they are responsible for this as much as I am. They put in many, many hours.

INTRODUCTION

In the summer of 1998, as our family traveled, talking about poems and the idea of a book of poems, we were suddenly struck by the thought that we had never heard a jump-rope rhyme with a Bible story as its basis. As the discussion continued, it grew into a plan to try to create some. During the next several weeks, the idea grew and grew, with the potential becoming clearer and clearer. Since I could remember jump-rope rhymes that I had played in my childhood, it seemed that Bible stories and principles learned in rhymes might also have a lifelong impact. My daughters, Jessica and Britni, and I began to write thoughts, ideas, and rhymes. As we refined the rhymes and shared them with others, we realized we were creating some fun and creative ways to learn Bible stories, verses, and principles.

God blessed this endeavor in ways that continue to amaze us—the way he continued to give us ideas for rhymes, the way he helped us find a publisher, and the way he enabled us to meet deadlines. Our hope and prayer is that this book can be used to enrich children's lives and to implant love for Christ through learning while playing these rhymes and games.

HOW TO USE THIS BOOK

This book is intended to be used as a supplement to any curriculum or Bible lesson you might be teaching. Because the games and activities reinforce many Bible stories, verses, and topics, we have provided the Scripture Index along with the Topical Index to make it easy for you to find just the activity you need.

After presenting your lesson to your class, use these games as

- an aid to memorization of a key verse,
- a time-filler after you have completed all your other activities,
- a substitute reinforcement activity when you need a more active game, or
- a reinforcement activity that can be done outdoors.

Jump-Rope Introduction

Jump-rope is a wonderful game—it's easy, cheap, fun, and great exercise. One person can play alone, or members of a large group can play together. There are innumerable rhymes to jump to and games to play. In group games, the goal is for the rope turners to work together to make the rope turn smoothly and for the jumpers to jump as long as possible without a miss. But even a miss is good in this game, because it gives someone else a chance to jump and allows the jumper time to rest for another turn.

Rope jumping has been around for thousands of years. In the eighteen hundreds, the English drank a drink called bitters, which was made from the female hop flower. Every year the people held a festival, and after they'd picked all the hops from the vine, the men, women, and children used the vine to jump rope.

During Victorian times, only boys jumped, and the game was very competitive. (Girls were thought to be too frail and fragile!) Unfortunately, children didn't have much time to jump, because many of them worked in factories or in fields. Often, though, children would carry a thin rope in their pockets for use at break time.

After child labor laws were passed, children had more time to play. Girls began to take over the game and make it more cooperative. The girls thought up all sorts of rhymes, rhythms, and actions to go with the jumps. When jump-rope became more of a recognized sport, boys began to rejoin.

Jump-rope is played all over the world, and many countries have their own name for the game. In Peru jump-rope is called El Reloj (The Clock). In Japan it is called Tobi–koshi (Jumping Over), and in China it is Tsuna Tobi (Rope Jumping). In some areas of China, there is a variation of the game called Rope Kicking in which a child runs up and kicks the rope with one foot, then turns around and kicks it with the other foot. If the child can do that, the rope holders raise the rope and the kicker tries again, until the rope is too high or the kicker misses the rope. (It's not as easy as it sounds!)

Most people have jumped rope when they were younger. Many even remember the rhymes they used to sing to the rhythm of the rope slapping the ground. People may remember using a variety of ropes. Some used their mothers' clotheslines, and others used barn ropes or horse lead ropes. Tying inner tubes together can even form a rope! In other countries children use grapevines, leather thongs, and twisted fibers knotted together.

Something special in the rhythm and rhyme of jump-rope chants make the rhymes stick around for generations. Turn the pages, and let rope jumping cement Bible stories in the minds of your students!

JUMP-ROPE RHYMES

Old Testament

Bible ABC's

DIRECTIONS:

Two "turners" each hold an end of the rope, a "jumper" stands near the middle, and the rest of the group line up behind the jumper. The turners swing the rope up in an arc over the jumper's head. As the rope comes down and nears the ground, the jumper jumps so that the rope can go under his or her feet. The turners will continue to swing the rope around so that the jumper can jump until he or she is tired or stops the rope. Each time the jumper jumps, call out a letter of the alphabet. When the jumper misses or stops, he or she must say the name of a biblical place, name, idea, or book of the Bible that begins with the letter that he or she stopped jumping on. Some suggestions are listed below:

A: Acts, Amos

B: Babylon, Bartholomew, baptism, Barnabas, believe, Bethlehem

C: 1 Chronicles, 2 Chronicles, Colossians, 1 Corinthians, 2 Corinthians, Christ

D: Daniel, Deuteronomy

E: Ecclesiastes, Ephesians, Esther, Exodus, Ezekiel, Ezra

F: Forgiveness, family, fasting, figs, Flood, faith, Father, fishermen

G: Genesis, Galatians

H: Habakkuk, Haggai, Hebrews, Hosea

I: Isaiah

J: James, Jeremiah, Job, Joel, John, 1 John, 2 John, 3 John, Joshua, Jude, Judges

K: 1 Kings, 2 Kings

L: Lamentations, Leviticus, Luke

M: Malachi, Mark, Matthew, Micah

N: Nahum, Nehemiah, Numbers

O: Obadiah

P: 1 Peter, 2 Peter, Philemon, Philippians, Proverbs, Psalm

Q: Queen Esther, Queen Jezebel, Queen of Sheba

R: Revelation, Romans, Ruth

S: 1 Samuel, 2 Samuel, Song of Solomon

T: 1 Thessalonians, 2 Thessalonians, 1 Timothy, 2 Timothy, Titus

U: Understanding, unity, universe, upright, useful

V: Valuable, vineyard, vision, voice

W: Wonderful, wisdom, wealth, white, wilderness, win, wine, Word (God's), worship, worthy

X: Xerxes (Queen Esther's husband)

Y: Yeast, yoke, youth, yarn

Z: Zacchaeus, Zebulun, Zephaniah, Zerubbabel, Zion

Creation

DIRECTIONS:

Choose two children to turn the rope as the group sings the following rhyme to the tune of "Mary Had a Little Lamb." As they begin the rhyme, the first child jumps in. At the end of the first verse, the child jumps out and the next child jumps in for the next verse. For younger children or for children with less experience jumping rope, have the turners stop turning at the end of each verse, so one child may move out of the jumping area and the next child may move in. If necessary, repeat the rhyme until everyone has had a turn to jump.

In the beginning, God created, God
   created, God created,
In the beginning God created
The heavens and the earth.

On the first day God made light, God
   made light, God made light.
On the first day God made light,
So there was night and day.

On the second day God made sky, God
   made sky, God made sky.
On the second day God made sky.
Now there's sky and water.

On the third day God made land, God
   made land, God made land.
On the third day God made land,
Creating sea and land.

On the fourth day God made stars, God
   made stars, God made stars.
On the fourth day God made stars,
Sun and moon and stars.

On the fifth day God made birds, God
   made birds, God made birds.
On the fifth day God made birds,
And God made fishes too.

On the sixth day God made animals, God
   made animals, God made animals.
On the sixth day God made animals,
And God made Adam and Eve.

On the seventh day God did rest, God did
   rest, God did rest.
On the seventh day God did rest,
And God said it was good.

Down in the Garden

DIRECTIONS:

Choose two children to hold the ends of the rope. Have one of those two wiggle the rope, slowly, on the ground so that it looks like a snake. As children begin the following rhyme, the first child will jump to the middle and put one foot on either side of the rope. The jumper should jump back and forth on each foot, to avoid touching the rope. When the jumper gets tired or the rope touches the jumper, the next child takes a turn. For a variation, have the jumper jump over the rope with both feet together.

Down in the garden,
Down by a tree,
God made Adam, then made Eve.
God said, "There's a certain tree,
Do not eat from it, you see."

Down in the garden,
Down by a tree,
The snake came a-crawlin' after Eve.
"Nothing bad will happen, wait and see.
Go ahead and eat from that old tree."

Down in the garden,
Down by a tree,
They tasted that fruit—Adam and Eve.
God called Adam, and Adam called Eve.
God said, "Why did you disobey me?"

Down in the garden,
Down by a tree,
Nothing is left for us to see.
Adam and Eve had to flee
When they ate from the tree.

SCRIPTURE REFERENCE

▼

Genesis 6-8

Noah, Noah

DIRECTIONS:

This rhyme can be used by a child jumping alone or by a group. For group play, have two children turn the rope and when a child jumps in, have everyone begin saying the rhyme. Count by twos until the jumper misses. Begin again with the next child.

Noah, Noah on a boat,
How many animals will you float?
(2, 4, 6, 8, …)

SCRIPTURE REFERENCE

▼

Genesis 11:1-9

Tower of Babel

DIRECTIONS:

This rhyme is a "call and answer" rhyme in which the jumper says something and then the turners say something back. Choose two children to turn the rope, and when the jumper jumps in, have him or her begin the first line. As the rhyme goes on, the turners will raise their hands slightly to raise the rope higher off the ground. They will continue to gradually raise it higher until the jumper can no longer jump over the rope, or until the end of the rhyme. Begin again with the next child.

TEACHER TIP
Be sure to explain the meaning of any words in this rhyme that your children might not be familiar with, such as the word "pity."

JUMPER: Let's build a tall, tall tower.
TURNERS: Tall enough to show our power.

JUMPER: How do we build it?
TURNERS: Big bricks filled it.

JUMPER: We will build a great city.
TURNERS: Great idea, no time for pity.

JUMPER: God has seen our prideful hearts.
TURNERS: He will change our language parts.

JUMPER: The Tower of Babel got us in trouble.
TURNERS: Put God first on the double.

Abraham and Isaac

DIRECTIONS:

For this rhyme, children will play Follow the Leader. Have two children turn the rope, and have all the others line up in single file. The first child in line will be the leader. He or she will jump in for the first verse and do an action such as touching the ground, touching his or her nose, or winking. At the end of the verse, the leader will then jump out on the other side. The other children will have to repeat the same action as they jump for one verse. Have the leader go to the end of the line, and begin with the next person in line as the new leader. Be sure to rotate turners so all children get a chance to jump.

Once a man named Abraham
Went with God to a distant land.

He had always wanted a son,
Then God promised Abraham one.

One day when he was very old,
He had a son as he was told.

God said, "Give to me your son."
Abraham knew it must be done.

Abraham took Isaac along,
Tied his son with rope so strong.

He was about to give his son,
When God said it needn't be done.

In the bushes, see a ram,
He will be the sacrifice lamb.

Since Abraham followed all God's plans,
He has fathered many lands.

Pharaoh

DIRECTIONS:

Have two children turn the rope. The rest of the children will form two lines near the middle of the rope. These groups will alternate saying the verses. The first person in the line will jump to the verse that his or her group says. At the end of the verse, that child will jump out and the first person in the other line will jump in.

(Group 1)
Pharaoh, Pharaoh, can it be?
God sent Moses, don't you see.
He has come to speak to thee.
You must set his people free.

(Group 2)
Pharaoh, Pharaoh, listen to me.
You must set God's people free.
How many signs must God show,
Before you'll let his people go?

(Group 1)
Changed from staff to snake instead.
It is just as Moses said.
Pharaoh, Pharaoh, the Nile is red.
It is just as Moses said.

(Group 2)
Frogs are landing in my bed.
It is just as Moses said.
There are gnats around my head.
It is just as Moses said.

(continued)

(Group 1)
There are flies upon my bread.
It is just as Moses said.
All my animals are now dead.
It is just as Moses said.

(Group 2)
On my body, sores did spread.
It is just as Moses said.
From the pounding hail we fled.
It is just as Moses said.

(Group 1)
Buzzing locusts 'round my head.
It is just as Moses said.
Now no light—not a shred.
It is just as Moses said.

(Group 2)
Over the door, the lamb's blood was
    spread.
Israel's sons are not dead.
Egypt's firstborn sons are dead.
It is just as Moses said.

(Group 1)
Pharaoh, Pharaoh, now you see,
The God of Abraham spoke to me.
You have let his people free.
Now they'll cross the big Red Sea.

Moses and the Israelites

Exodus
12:31-42;
13:17–14:31;
16:1–17:7;
20:1-21;
Joshua 3–4

DIRECTIONS:

This game provides more of a challenge. Choose two children to turn the rope, and have the rest of the children form groups of three. As the entire group begins singing the rhyme to the tune of "On the Road Again," the first group of three will hold hands and then jump in. When kids have finished the first verse, the group will jump out and the next group of three will jump in. If you do not have enough children to form more groups of three, rotate the children in the group with the turners so all children get a chance to jump.

On the trail again.
I just can't believe we're on the trail
    again!
For forty years we wandered.
We kicked the dust till night.
I just can't believe we're on the trail
    again!

We crossed the big Red Sea.
Before Pharaoh's army, we crossed the
    big Red Sea.
The Ten Commandments, they became
    our law.
I just can't believe we crossed the big
    Red Sea.

We have walked for miles.
I just can't believe we've walked so many
    miles.
Water from a rock and manna from the
    sky.
I just can't believe we've walked so many
    miles.

We've reached the promised land.
I just can't believe we've reached the
    promised land.
A land of milk and honey, where God
    will provide.
We are glad we're in the promised land.

The Ten Commandments

SCRIPTURE
REFERENCE
▼

Exodus 20:1-21;
Deuteronomy
5:7-21

DIRECTIONS:

Only one child will be the turner for this game. Have the child spin the rope in a circle so the rope is only a few inches above the ground. As the turner calls out each number, a new child will jump in. The children will respond to the number by saying the commandment and jumping the rope when it comes around to where they stand. At the end all ten children will jump out and shout the numbers one through ten. If you play with a smaller group of children, you may need to assign more than one commandment to some of the children.

Name the Ten Commandments,
Name them one by one.

TURNER: One
CHILDREN: I will have no other God.

TURNER: Two
CHILDREN: I will not make any idols.

TURNER: Three
CHILDREN: I will respect God's name.

TURNER: Four
CHILDREN: I will keep the Lord's day holy.

TURNER: Five
CHILDREN: I will obey mom and dad.

The first set of five are done,
Aren't you just having fun?

TURNER: Six
CHILDREN: I will not kill anyone.

TURNER: Seven
CHILDREN: I will stay faithful to the one I marry.

TURNER: Eight
CHILDREN: I will not steal anything.

TURNER: Nine
CHILDREN: I will not tell any lies.

TURNER: Ten
CHILDREN: I will not want what you have.

Jump out and give a shout!

Balaam

SCRIPTURE
REFERENCE
▼

Numbers
22:21-38

DIRECTIONS:

Two children will turn the rope, and one child will jump in as the rhyme begins. On the third line, have another child jump in to be the angel, and then on the fifth line, have a third child jump in. All three will jump until the end of the rhyme. Have different children turn the rope, and begin again.

Balaam was being a stubborn man.
He wasn't paying attention to God's plan.

(Another child jumps in.)
There was an angel in his way,
So from the trail his donkey did stray.

(Another child jumps in.)
The frightened donkey made a stop,
And Balaam gave it quite a bop.

The little donkey then did talk,
And Baalam's eyes did really pop.

(continued)

The Lord then opened Balaam's eyes,
Told him, "This path is not wise."

"Continue on, but change your way,
And say just what God says to say."

Joshua's Battle

DIRECTIONS:

With two turners, have a child jump in as the group begins saying the rhyme. At the end of the second verse, the jumper must jump out, run around the turners, and then jump back in. At the end of the rhyme, the jumper must jump out and touch the ground. Begin again with another jumper. Be sure to allow the turners a chance to jump also.

Joshua fought the battle of Jericho,
Jericho.

Around the wall they must go,
They must go.
(Jumper jumps out and runs around turners, then jumps back in.)

For seven days in a row,
In a row.

1, 2, 3, 4, 5, 6, 7

On the seventh day the trumpet did blow,
the trumpet did blow.

And the walls they came a-tumbling down,
To the ground.
(Jumper jumps out and touches the ground.)

Gideon

DIRECTIONS:

Line up all the children in single file, with two children turning the rope. As the group begins the rhyme, the turners turn the rope, and at the end of each line, the other children must run all the way through the turning rope without being touched. If a child is touched, he or she is out. Repeat the rhyme as necessary.

"Trust in me is the key,"
Says the Lord to Gideon and me.
He only needs a small army.
To make the Midianites flee.

All those men who are not scared,
All those men who are prepared,
Drinking water from the hand,
Will show you who is in your band.

Went to the Midianite camp,
With their jars and with their lamps.
They made noise and lit their lights,
Which gave the Midianites a great fright.

They woke up to a dreadful noise.
And each other they did destroy.
Without Gideon using his hand,
God protected Israel's land.

Ruth and Boaz

SCRIPTURE REFERENCE

▼

Ruth 1–4

DIRECTIONS:

Pairs of children will jump in for each verse of the rhyme and will perform an action before jumping out. The entire group will say the rhyme as two children turn the rope. Be sure to let children trade roles so that all children get a chance to jump.

(Hold hands while jumping.)
Ruth and Naomi from another land,
Walked across the desert hand in hand.
(Jump out.)

Ruth worked hard to get food,
But she had the right attitude.
(Touch the ground before jumping out.)

(Pretend to eat while jumping.)
Boaz said, "Please eat with me,
You will be great company."
(Jump out.)

(Shake fingers at each other while jumping.)
Naomi said, "You need a home,
You should not be all alone."
(Jump out.)

Then Boaz asked for Ruth's hand.
It was all part of God's great plan.
(Hold hands while jumping out.)

Samuel

SCRIPTURE REFERENCE

▼

1 Samuel 1, 3

DIRECTIONS:

Have two children turn the rope, and have the rest of the group line up near the middle of the rope. As children begin the rhyme, have the first child jump in. At the end of each verse, the child must jump and turn around as he or she jumps for each letter that is said. Then the child jumps out, and a new child jumps in for the next verse. Allow the children turning the rope to also have a turn jumping.

Hannah had always wanted a son,
Because the Lord had given her none.
God gave Hannah a son, Samuel.
(Jump and turn around on each letter.)
S-A-M-U-E-L
(Jump out.)

He was a child unlike any other.
Given back to God by his mother.
Living in the temple with Eli.
(Jump and turn around on each letter.)
E-L-I
(Jump out.)

Three times God did call one night.
That gave Samuel a great big fright.
God said Eli and his sons would die.
(Jump and turn around on each letter.)
1, 2, 3
(Jump out.)

God gave Samuel the words to tell
That helped Israel very well.
Samuel spoke God's word to Israel.
(Jump and turn around on each letter.)
I-S-R-A-E-L
(Jump out.)

Elijah

DIRECTIONS:

Have two children turn the rope for this rhyme. As you begin the rhyme, have the first child jump in for the first line, and have a different child jump for each line. Be sure to allow the children turning the rope to have a chance to jump.

One, one: Elijah's on the run.
Two, two: God said ravens will feed you.
Three, three: The widow's cakes will feed thee.
Four, four: The widow's son lived once more.

Five, five: For God Elijah did strive.
Six, six: God burned the bull, stones, and sticks.
Seven, seven: Elijah took a chariot to heaven.

Esther

DIRECTIONS:

As two children turn the rope, let a different child jump for each verse. All the children should say the rhyme together. After several children have jumped, choose new children to turn the rope so that all the children get a chance to jump.

Mordecai, Mordecai,
Do your duty.
Here comes Esther,
The Jewish beauty.
She's found favor before royalty.
She will soon be queen, you see.
(Jump out and let another child jump in.)

Esther, Esther,
Do your duty.
You're our favorite
Jewish beauty.
Save your people, hear their cry.
Listen to cousin Mordecai!
(Jump out and let another child jump in.)

Xerxes, Xerxes,
Do your duty.
Here comes Esther,
The Jewish beauty.
You're the king, what will you do?
To Esther's people, please be true.
(Jump out and let another child jump in.)

Israel, Israel,
She did her duty.
It was Esther,
The Jewish beauty.
She talked to the king, so you'll not die.
Haman will hang, not Mordecai.

Job

DIRECTIONS:

Choose two children to turn the rope while the rest of the group lines up for a turn to jump. Have the jumper stand near the middle of the rope. The turners swing the rope back and forth. Each time they swing the rope, it should go higher until the rope goes all the way over. Then they'll turn the rope as they normally would. The jumper will then jump until the end of the rhyme. Begin the rhyme again with a different child as the jumper, making sure you also choose different children to turn the rope.

Job was God's man,
And Satan had a plan.
Satan thought he was so grand,
That he would ruin all Job's land.
(Rope starts going over jumper's head.)

Satan thought that he would win.
He killed all of Job's children,

Put big sores upon Job's skin.
But faithful Job did not give in.

Job, he had some unkind friends.
Advice to Job they did send.
On the Lord, Job learned to depend.
God still is faithful to the end.

> **TEACHER TIP**
> Be sure to explain the meaning of any words your children might not be familiar with, such as "advice" or "depend."

Count Your Blessings

DIRECTIONS:

With two children turning the rope and the rest lined up single file, the group will say the rhyme. When they've finished, each child will run in and say a blessing in their life as they jump, and then run out. The rest of the children will do the same. As a variation to this, each child may have a turn running in and counting until he or she misses.

Every day and so many more. . .
I count my blessings from the Lord.

How many blessings did I count?
(Count or name your blessings.)

Psalm 119:105

DIRECTIONS:

This jumping chant is a "call and response" game. Choose two children to turn the rope, and the rest will take turns jumping. After the turners say their part, the rest of the group will spell the word and the jumper will jump one time for each letter. Have the child turn a quarter turn with each jump. A different child will jump for each word.

TURNERS: The Bible
JUMPER: B-I-B-L-E
TURNERS: is a lamp
JUMPER: L-A-M-P

TURNERS: to my feet and a light
JUMPER: L-I-G-H-T
TURNERS: for my path.
JUMPER: P-A-T-H.

Six Words of Wisdom

DIRECTIONS:

Only one person is needed to turn the rope for this chant. Assign each of the letters to a different child. When the turner says a letter, he or she will drop the rope to the ground and spin in circles, and the person who was assigned that letter will jump in, say his or her response, and jump out. The jumpers must try not to touch the rope. Allow different children a chance to turn the rope.

W —With a guarded heart, face the world.

I —Instruction must be treasured.

S —Store God's commandments in your heart.

D —Delight the Lord with honesty.

O —Obedience is the key.

M —Make sure you follow God's path.

Proverbs 3:5-6

DIRECTIONS:

Have two children turn the rope. Start the rhyme after the jumper is in and ready. The jumper will jump for the entire verse. As a variation, a different child may jump for each line of the verse. Allow different children to have a turn turning the rope so all children get a chance to jump.

Trust, trust, trust the Lord with
All, all, all your heart and
Lean, lean, lean not on your
Own, own, own understanding.

Seek, seek, seek his will in
All, all, all you do and
He, He, He will direct your
Path, path, path.

Shadrach, Meshach, and Abednego

DIRECTIONS:

Choose two children to turn the ropes. Also choose children to be Shadrach, Meshach, Abednego, the king, and the angel. All the other children may be the guards. When the rhyme begins, have Shadrach, Meshach, and Abednego jump in. Have the king jump in on the second verse and gently pretend to push the other three as they jump out. On verse four have the guards gently push the three men back in and have the king jump out. On the next verse, have the angel jump in. On the last verse, have Shadrach, Meshach, and Abednego jump out again. The angel will continue to jump until the end of the rhyme.

(Shadrach, Meshach, and Abednego jump in.)

Shadrach, Meshach, and Abednego
Three served a mighty king, oh no.

(The King jumps in.)
The king said, "All must bow to me,"
"We'll bow to God!" said the three.
(Shadrach, Meshach, and Abednego jump out.)

The king said throw them in the fire,
The guards said, "If it please you, sire."

(King jumps out. Shadrach, Meshach and Abednego jump in.)

All three went into the fire.
The hot flames burned higher and higher.

(The angel jumps in.)
Suddenly the fire held four.
An angel sent by the Lord.

(Shadrach, Meshach, and Abednego jump out.)
The king said, "You three men, come out.
Your God's mighty, there's no doubt!"

Daniel in the Lions' Den

SCRIPTURE REFERENCE
▼
Daniel 6

DIRECTIONS:
    With two children turning the rope, lead the rest of the group in saying the rhyme. The children will take turns trying to jump throughout the whole rhyme. Rotate which children turn the rope so that everyone gets a chance to jump.

Daniel was down in the lions' den,
Because he would not pray to men.
But Daniel was not afraid,
Of these creatures God had made.

In the morning to the king's great joy,
Daniel had not been destroyed.
The king found out that God was strong,
Daniel had been right all along.

Jonah

SCRIPTURE REFERENCE
▼
Jonah 1–4

DIRECTIONS:
    Have two children turn the rope, and direct everyone else to line up single file. As you lead the rhyme, the children must take turns running through the spinning rope, without jumping or being touched by the rope. If a child succeeds, then he or she will line up again on the opposite side of the rope. If not, the child will go to the end of the line to try again. Continue repeating the rhyme as necessary. The first two children to get through the rope will become the turners for the next round.

Jonah, Jonah have you heard?
God wants you to spread the word!
In Nineveh—they need to know,
But Jonah said, "No, I won't go!"
Jonah, Jonah caught a ship
Under the deck he did slip.

A big storm came upon the ship,
So Jonah had to take a dip.
Jonah, Jonah in the whale,
For three days he did wail.
Then to Nineveh he did sail,
Finally there he told the tale.

JUMP-ROPE RHYMES

New Testament

Joseph and Mary

DIRECTIONS:

Have children form the following groups: two children to turn the rope, two to be Joseph and Mary, three to be shepherds, three to be wise men, and the remainder can be children. Joseph and Mary will jump in together for the first verse and follow the directions indicated following the verse. For the second verse, the shepherds will jump in. Have the wise men jump in together for the third verse. For the last verse, have the children jump in. If you have a large group, choose only two children to jump to the last verse and have the rest of the group jump to the rhyme the next time. For a smaller group, children may jump to more than one verse. Be sure to let children take turns turning the rope so that everyone gets a chance to jump.

(Mary and Joseph jump in.)

Joseph and Mary, Joseph and Mary, came to town.

Joseph and Mary, Joseph and Mary, slept on the ground. *(Touch the ground.)*

Joseph and Mary, Joseph and Mary, cows did moo. *(Make mooing sounds.)*

Joseph and Mary, Joseph and Mary, Jesus was born, too.

(Mary and Joseph jump out.)

(Shepherds jump in.)

Shepherds, shepherds, look in the air. *(Look up.)*

Shepherds, shepherds, see the angels singing there.

Shepherds, shepherds, who went that night,

Shepherds, shepherds, bowed at such a sight. *(Bow slightly while jumping.)*

(Shepherds jump out.)

(Wise men jump in.)

Wise men, wise men, who followed the light,

Wise men, wise men, found him that night.

Wise men, wise men, with gifts so rare,

Wise men, wise men, present them there.

(Hold out hands, palms up, as if presenting a gift while jumping. Then jump out.)

(Children jump in.)

Children, children, follow the light. *(Turn half turn.)*

Children, children, do what's right.

Children, children, choose God's way. *(Turn half turn.)*

Children, children, do it today.

Herod, Herod

DIRECTIONS:

Choose one child to be Herod, who will jump for all verses. Have a different child jump with Herod for each verse. Two children will turn the rope. Have Herod and the first child jump in when the rhyme begins. Repeat the rhyme as often as needed to allow all children a chance to jump.

(Herod and first child begin jumping.)
Herod, Herod, you've been dreaming.

Why in the world have you been scheming?

Your kingdom's threatened, by a child,
And you're not taking it very mild.
(Child exits.)

(Next child jumps in.)
Herod, Herod, what's wrong with you?
Killing all boys under two.
Joseph found out, they're on the trail.

This plan of yours is gonna fail!
(Child exits.)

(Next child jumps in.)
Herod, Herod, you've been scheming,
But I'm afraid you're only dreaming.
Jesus is gone from your lands.
So much for your wicked plan!

Jesus Is My Name

SCRIPTURE REFERENCE

Matthew 1:18-25; 27:33–28:15; Mark 2:1-12; 15:21–16:20; Luke 1:26-45; 2:41-52; 4–5; 23:26–24:12; John 19:17–20:9

DIRECTIONS:

A different child will jump for each verse while two children turn the rope. All the children will say the rhyme and shout the last line in each verse. Allow different children to turn the rope so that all children get a chance to jump.

I was born in Bethlehem.
Do you know who I am?
Jesus is my name.

In the temple left behind,
So, my parents couldn't find.
Jesus is my name.

Don't you know, I healed the lame.
I did not want any fame.
Jesus is my name.

For your sins, I had to die.
For this reason, I did cry.
Jesus is my name.

On the third day, I did raise,
So now, give God all the praise.
Jesus is my name.

Jesus by the Sea

SCRIPTURE REFERENCE

Matthew 4:18-22; Mark 1:16-20; Luke 5:1-11; John 1:35-42

DIRECTIONS:

Choose two children to turn the rope and the rest of the children will take turns jumping. Have a child jump in when the rhyme begins. At the end of the rhyme, everyone will keep counting until the jumper makes a mistake and stops the rope. The next child will then start at the beginning of the rhyme. Allow the turners also to have a chance to jump.

Jesus went fishing down by the sea.
He called up fisherman one, two, three.
Now he's calling for you and me.

How many of us will there be?
   (1, 2, 3, 4, ...)

BeAttitudes

Matthew 5:3-10

DIRECTIONS:

Start with a child standing near the center of the rope and two children turning the rope. For the first part of each line, the turners will turn the rope one time in one direction, and for the second half of each line, they will turn it in the opposite direction. Choose different children to be rope turners so everyone gets a chance to jump. Repeat the verse as often as needed for all children to have a chance to jump.

Be humble, don't stumble.
Be meek, when you speak.
Be kind, please mind.

Be good, do as you should.
Be peaceful and quiet, don't start a riot.
Be true, people count on you!

Matthew 7:7-9

Matthew 7:7-9

DIRECTIONS:

Start by having two children turn the rope. They will swing the rope back and forth, without turning it all the way overhead. They'll keep swinging the rope higher to each side, until the rope goes all the way over the top. Then they'll turn the rope as they normally would. As the group says the rhyme, one child will jump throughout the entire rhyme. Then the next child will jump. Be sure to allow different children to turn the rope so that everyone gets a chance to jump.

I asked and he gave.
I looked and I found.
I knocked, and he opened the door with
   a wave. *(Rope goes overhead.)*

He was glad I asked.
He was glad I looked.
He was glad I knocked, and I'm content
   at last.

Good Foundations

*Matthew
7:24-27*

DIRECTIONS:

Two children will alternate jumping to the verses of this rhyme—one as the fool, one as the wise man—as two children turn the rope. Repeat the verse for the next two children to jump, being sure that children who turn the rope get a chance to jump.

There was a wise man and a fool.
The fool thought building on sand was cool.

The wise man knew that rock was better.

The house would stand, no matter the
   weather.

Then down came a very heavy rain,

And the fool's house crashed down the drain!

The wise man's house was there at dawn,

When the weather cleared and the rain was gone.

So build your life on God, who's true.
He'll be there your whole life through!

Jairus' Daughter

SCRIPTURE REFERENCE
▼

Matthew 9:18-26;
Mark 5:21-43;
Luke 8:40-56

DIRECTIONS:

Have all of the children line up single file, and choose two to turn the rope. As the group begins saying the rhyme, for each line, have one person jump in, jump once, and then jump out.

Jairus, Jairus,
Your daughter's near dead.
Please bring Jesus to her bed.

In walked Jesus,
In walked the mother,
In walked Peter, James, and John his brother.

Jesus saw the girl.
He said, "Get up."
"Give her food to eat and a drink from a cup."

Out walked Jesus,
Out walked the mother,
Out walked Peter, James, and John his brother.

The Twelve Disciples

SCRIPTURE REFERENCE
▼

Matthew 10:2-4;
Mark 3:16-19;
Luke 6:14-16

DIRECTIONS:

The apostles' names will be sung to the tune of "Sailing, Sailing" as two children turn the rope. After the group has sung the names, one child will jump in for the next line ("They are Jesus' disciples"), jumping once for each number. Then that child will jump out. Next have two children jump in to say, "They did preach the gospel," jumping once for each number. Then have them jump out. For the last line, have three children jump in, jump to the numbers, and then jump out at the end.

Matthew, Philip, Peter, and Thomas, too.
Judas, John—the list goes on!
James and Bartholomew,
Simon, Andrew, don't forget Thaddaeus.
And we must remember James, the son of Alphaeous.

(One child jumps in.)

They are Jesus' disciples. *(Child counts to twelve by ones, then jumps out. Two other children jump in.)*
They did preach the gospel. *(Children count to twelve by twos, then jump out. Three other children jump in.)*
They did many miracles. *(Children count to twelve by threes, then jump out.)*

Five Loaves and Two Fish

SCRIPTURE REFERENCE

▼

Matthew 14:13-21;
Mark 6:30-44;
Luke 9:10-17;
John 6:1-13

DIRECTIONS:

Choose one child to jump for the entire rhyme while two others turn the rope. Have the jumper jump in when the group begins saying the rhyme. At the end, keep counting until the jumper makes a mistake. Repeat the rhyme so that each child has a chance to jump.

Jesus fed 5,000 and more,
While he was preaching by the shore.

Five loaves and two fish,
How many pieces do you wish?
(1, 2, 3, 4, ...)

The Great Story

SCRIPTURE REFERENCE

▼

Matthew 27:33–28:15;
Mark 15:21–16:20;
Luke 23:26–24:12;
John 19:17–20:9

DIRECTIONS:

One child will jump for the entire rhyme, and two will turn the rope. Have the jumper jump in when the group begins saying the rhyme. At the end, keep counting until the jumper misses or becomes tired. Repeat the rhyme so that each child gets a chance to jump.

Jesus came 'cause he loves me.
Died on a cross for all to see.
With his death my sins were gone.
On the third day he rose at dawn.
Now we tell this awesome story.

Full of wonder and full of glory.
People need to know him well.
How many people will we tell?
   (1, 2, 3, 4, ...)

Ten Virgins Parable

SCRIPTURE REFERENCE

▼

Matthew 25:1-13

DIRECTIONS:

Choose two children to turn the rope, and have all of the other children line up single-file. As the rhyme begins, a child will jump in, jump until the end of the rhyme, and jump out. Repeat the rhyme as needed so that all children get a chance to jump.

A cry rang out at midnight,
The bridegroom is here.

Ten virgins went to meet him,
But the night was not clear.

1, 2, 3, 4, 5, 6, 7, 8, 9, 10
Ten took their lamps and trimmed them,
But only five did glow.

1, 2, 3, 4, 5

And to the wedding banquet,
With my Lord, they did go.

Jesus the bridegroom comes for me,
Oh, how happy we will be.

The Lost Coin

SCRIPTURE REFERENCE ▼

Luke 15:8-10

DIRECTIONS:

This rhyme is sung to the tune of "Little Bo Peep." Only one person will be the turner for this rhyme. All the other children will stand in a circle around the turner. Have the turner spin the rope over his or her head. When the group begins the rhyme, the turner will drop the rope and spin it on the ground by turning in circles. Then have all the jumpers jump forward and jump every time the rope comes around to where they stand.

There was a woman who lost her coin
And didn't know where to find it.
She looked around, checked the ground,
And rejoiced when she had found it.

Without my Jesus, I was lost.
And life was sad and lonely.
But now I'm found, I'm safe and sound,
'Cause Jesus showed he loves me.

The Prodigal Son

SCRIPTURE REFERENCE ▼

Luke 15:11-32

DIRECTIONS:

A different child will jump for each verse of this rhyme as two children turn the rope. Repeat the rhyme as needed for each child to have a turn to jump.

Once a man had a son
Who only wanted to have fun.
So from home, he did run.

To the city, he did go.
There he partied—spent his dough!
He wasn't very smart, oh, no!

He soon ran out of money,
Feeding pigs was not funny.
His old life looked very sunny.

Now this hungry, sorry son,
Who only wanted to have fun,
Into his father's arms did run.

And when we, like this son,
Turn from the wrong things we've done,
Into God's arms we can run.

John 3:16

SCRIPTURE REFERENCE ▼

John 3:16

DIRECTIONS:

One child will jump for the entire rhyme as two children turn the rope. At the end of the rhyme, continue to spell "L-I-F-E," each time saying the letters more quickly and turning the rope more quickly until the jumper can no longer jump. Repeat this rhyme so that each child gets a chance to jump.

For God so loved the world,
That he gave his only Son.
That whoever believes in him

Will not die, but have
Everlasting L-I-F-E.

Many Rooms

DIRECTIONS:

Choose two children to turn the rope. Children will take turns jumping for the entire rhyme. For each line of this rhyme, children will turn the rope in opposite directions. Start with the jumper standing near the center of the rope, or have the jumper attempt to jump in. As the group begins saying the rhyme, swing the rope up and over one way as the jumper jumps over it, and then turn the rope back the other way, up and over, as the jumper jumps over it. Repeat for the rest of the rhyme until the last line, when the turners will keep turning in the same direction, counting aloud until the jumper misses. Repeat the rhyme so that all children get a chance to jump.

Way up in heaven,
Beyond eternity,
Jesus has prepared a mansion for me.
He told me,

I told you.
Now the rest is up to you.
How many rooms will there be?
(1, 2, 3, 4, ...)

John 14:6

DIRECTIONS:

Three children will jump for this chant as two children turn the rope. The first child will jump in as the rhyme begins, jumping for the first line. That child will leave, and a second child will jump for the next line. The second child will leave at the end of the second line, and the third child will jump for the third line. Kids should jump one time for each letter at the end of each line. For the last two lines, have all three children jump together and repeat the lines until the children get tired or miss. Repeat with a different group of three children, being sure to choose different children to turn the rope so everyone gets a chance to jump.

(Child jumps in.)
I am the way W-A-Y,
(Child jumps out.)

(Second child jumps in.)
The truth T-R-U-T-H,
(Second child jumps out.)

(Third child jumps in.)
And the life L-I-F-E.
(Third child jumps out.)

(All three children jump in.)
W-A-Y, T-R-U-T-H, L-I-F-E,
Way truth and life.
(All three children jump out.)

One, Two, Three, Four

SCRIPTURE
REFERENCE
▼
*Matthew
25:1-13;
28:16-20;
John 14:6;
1 Thessalonians
4:13-18*

DIRECTIONS:

One child will begin jumping to the rhyme as two children turn the rope. A second child will jump in on the second line, a third child on the third line, and a fourth child will jump in on the fourth line. At the end, all four children will be jumping rope. Repeat the rhyme, allowing four different children to jump to the rhyme. Be sure to rotate which children turn the rope so that all children get a chance to jump.

One way to heaven,
Two to learn the way,

Three to tell a friend,
Four to be ready for the day.

H - O - P - E

SCRIPTURE
REFERENCE
▼
*Romans
8:24-25;
1 Timothy 4:10*

DIRECTIONS:

Two children will be turners, and children will jump one at a time. As the jumper jumps in, the group will say the rhyme. At the end, the group will repeatedly spell the word "H-O-P-E," with the jumper jumping once for each letter. When the jumper misses, follow the directions for the letter the jumper missed on.

H-O-P-E
This is what God gives me.

H: *High wire—Turn the rope, but don't let it touch the ground when it comes around. At its lowest point, it should be at least three inches above the ground. The jumper will jump until he or she cannot jump any longer, and then start all over with the next child.*

O: *Over—Swing the rope back and forth, but do not turn it all the way around. The* *jumper will jump over the rope repeatedly until he or she misses or is tired. Then start again with the next child.*

P: *Peppers—Turn the rope as fast as you can. The jumper will jump until he or she misses. Then start again with the next child.*

E: *Eyes shut—The jumper will jump with his or her eyes shut until the jumper misses. Then start again with the next child.*

Love Is

SCRIPTURE
REFERENCE
▼
*1 Corinthians
13:4-8*

DIRECTIONS:

Two children will be the turners, and children will jump, two at a time, holding hands. After each pair has sung the rhyme, begin again with new jumpers and new turners.

Love is patient, love is kind.
Love isn't rude or jealous you'll find!

Love does not make harsh demands.
Love is cool, love's not mad.

Love protects and hopes and trusts.
Love doesn't ever, ever, ever give up.

Fruit of the Spirit

SCRIPTURE REFERENCE ▼

Galatians 5:22-23

DIRECTIONS:

Have two children turn the rope while one child jumps. Everyone will say the first line and then repeats the list until the jumper can no longer jump. Repeat with the next jumper. Be sure to allow turners to be jumpers also.

Get into the act of the fruit of the Spirit.
Love
Joy
Peace
Patience
Kindness
Goodness
Faithfulness
Gentleness
Self-control

Ephesians 4:32

SCRIPTURE REFERENCE ▼

Ephesians 4:32

DIRECTIONS:

The children will form two groups, one on each side of the rope. Choose one child from each group to be turners. One child at a time will jump for the entire rhyme. When the first jumper jumps in, one group will say the first part of the line and the jumper will jump facing that group. The other group members will say the second half of the line, and the jumper will turn to face them. Repeat for the rest of the rhyme. Begin again with a new jumper from the other group, and choose different children to be the turners.

(Jumper faces first group as they call out.)
God rules—
(Jumper faces second group as they call out.)
Kindness rules.
(Jumper faces first group as they call out.)
Please don't fight—
(Jumper faces second group as they call out.)
That's not right.

(Jumper faces first group as they call out.)
Don't compete—
(Jumper faces second group as they call out.)
That's not neat.
(Jumper faces first group as they call out.)
Forgive each other—
(Jumper faces second group as they call out.)
Let's be sweet.

The Armor of God

SCRIPTURE REFERENCE
▼
Ephesians 6:10-18

DIRECTIONS:

One child at a time will jump to this rhyme while two children turn the rope. The group first says the rhyme and then the list as the jumper jumps. Keep repeating the list until the jumper misses. When the jumper stops, see whether he or she can explain the word he or she missed (as suggested below).

I'm gonna put on the armor of the Lord
From the helmet to the sword.

Helmet
Belt
Breastplate of Righteousness
Shoes
Shield
Sword

Belt of truth—so you know Satan's lies
Breastplate of righteousness—to protect our hearts from Satan's attack
Shoes of readiness—so we can tell others about Jesus
Shield of faith—to protect from Satan's evil arrows, Satan's lies and temptations
Helmet of salvation—to protect our minds from doubt
Sword of the Spirit—which is the Bible, to help us conquer sin

Philippians 4:13

SCRIPTURE REFERENCE
▼
Philippians 4:13

DIRECTIONS:

Two children will turn the rope, and one child at a time will jump to the entire rhyme. As the entire group says the rhyme, the jumper will jump toward one of the turners. When the jumper gets too close to a turner, have him or her turn around and move toward the other jumper. Continue the counting at the end until the jumper cannot jump any longer. Start over with a new jumper and new turners.

With the help of my Lord,
Any river I can ford.
I can walk any length,
By the power of his strength.

How far will I walk? (1 foot, 2 feet, 3 feet, …)

> **TEACHER TIP**
> This rhyme contains some words that may need to be explained to your children. Be sure they understand the word "ford."

1 Peter 5:7

SCRIPTURE REFERENCE
▼
1 Peter 5:7

DIRECTIONS:

For this game, one child at a time will jump for the rhyme as two children turn the rope. Have the jumper jump in as the group begins saying the rhyme. When the rhyme comes to "C-A-R-E-S," the turners should swing the rope back and forth instead of overhead in a circle. Repeat for the next child, being sure to choose new turners occasionally so that all children get a chance to jump.

Cast all your C-A-R-E-S
On God, because he

C-A-R-E-S for you.

SCRIPTURE
REFERENCE
▼

Matthew
27:33–28:15;
Mark
15:21–16:20;
Luke
23:26–24:12;
John 19:17–20:9

Two, Four, Six, Eight

DIRECTIONS:

One child will jump for each verse, and two will be turners. Have one jumper jump in, and have the group begin the rhyme. For the first two lines of each verse, have the jumper cross his or her legs in the air, then land, then jump up and uncross them. For the next two lines in each verse, have the jumper jump especially high, then squat, then jump out. Repeat the rhyme as needed. Be sure to allow the turners a chance to jump.

2, 4, 6, 8,
Our God is really great.
Up, down, in, out,
Unto the lord we shout.

C-H-R-I-S-T
He's the one who loves me.

Look around, touch the ground,
You were lost, but now you're found.

1, 2, 3, 4,
He'll love us forevermore.
Under, over, through, across,
Jesus showed his love on the cross.

Not Last Night, But the Night Before

SCRIPTURE
REFERENCE
▼

Revelation 3:20

DIRECTIONS:

Choose one child at a time to be a jumper and two children to be the turners. As the jumper jumps in, begin the rhyme. When the rhyme reaches the part "as I called out," have the jumper call out the name of another child in the group who is not turning. That child will come in, jump once, and then jump out on the other side. The jumper should do the same for all the other children in the group. When kids have finished the rhyme, begin the rhyme again with a new child as the first jumper and two new children as turners.

Not last night, but the night before,
Jesus came a knockin' at my door.
As I called out,
(One at a time, call out the names of children while jumping.)

He came in,
And I'll never be the same again.

CHINESE JUMP-ROPE

C hinese jump-rope, called Tio pi Jin in China, is played with a circular stretchy rope and is another popular form of rope jumping in the United States and other areas of the world.

Chinese jump-rope became popular in the United States in the 1960s and is again gaining popularity. Usually two children stand inside the rope, forming a rectangle. This is called the basic position.

Chinese jump-rope games are made up of a series of various jumps and hops, such as straddling the ropes, jumping inside, making a diamond, or doing a bunny hop. Many combinations and rhymes give the game interest and energy. If a player can complete all the moves in a game, the rope is moved up to provide more challenge. A player misses if he or she lands on the rope, lands in the wrong place, or gets tangled up when trying to jump out.

You can use these rhymes and actions to help your kids remember important Bible lessons, truths, and verses. Your kids may use them as a fun way to share God's truth with others. It will help to practice many of the moves before you try to do them with the rhymes.

Abraham

DIRECTIONS:

Abraham requires at least three players. Have two children form the basic position. The third child will complete a series of six jumps for each verse of the rhyme. The jumper will begin by standing at one side of the rectangle, facing one of the children holding the rope. He or she will do the first four moves for the first line of the verse, and the final two moves on the second line of the verse. For each verse change jumpers.

◼ Abraham, Abraham had a son.
1   2   3   4

1
Jump and land straddling nearer side rope.

2
Jump and land straddling the other side rope.

3
Jump and land inside the rectangle.

4
Jump and land straddling the rectangle.

◼ He was Isaac, the promised one.
5   6a   6b

5
Jump and land on the ropes and then jump and land off the ropes straddling the rectangle.

6a
Do a twistie. To do this, squeeze feet together with ropes between.

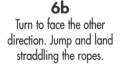
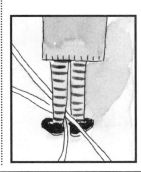

6b
Turn to face the other direction. Jump and land straddling the ropes.

◼ Isaac, Isaac your only son, *(Repeat first four moves.)*
◼ Give him to God, it must be done. *(Repeat last two moves.)*

■ **Angel, Angel stop Abraham's hand,** *(Repeat first four moves.)*
■ **Provide a ram for the stand.** *(Repeat last two moves.)*

■ **Children, children of Abraham,** *(Repeat first four moves.)*
■ **As God promised, filled the land.** *(Repeat last two moves.)*

Psalm 23

**SCRIPTURE
REFERENCE**

▼

Psalm 23

This game requires at least three players. Have two children form the basic position. Each of the following steps will be performed to one line of the rhyme. The jumper will begin by facing one of the children holding the rope, with the rope on the jumper's left side.

■ **The Lord is my shepherd.**

Place right foot on the nearest side rope. Then put left foot on the other side rope so that jumper is standing on the ropes with legs crossed. Jump off so the ropes are to the jumper's right side.

■ **He gives me all I need.**

Jump and land straddling nearer side rope. Jump and land with feet straddling the other rope. Run around the person holding the rope that you are facing to the side of the rope you began on.

■ **He always gives me strength.**

Face the other person holding the rope and place right foot on the nearest side rope. Then put left foot on the other side rope. Jump off so the ropes are to the jumper's right side.

(continued)

■ He shows me where to walk.

Stand with your back to the ropes. Jump toward the ropes, turning while jumping. Land on the other side of both ropes with back to the ropes.

■ With him I have no fear.

Face the ropes, and place toes just under the near rope.

Jump, keeping the near rope over your feet, and land over the far rope.

Jump up letting the rope slip off your feet.

■ He's with me and comforts me.

Repeat the jumps from the previous line, going the other direction.

■ I will live with him always.

Turn your back to the ropes. Jump toward the ropes, turning while jumping. Land on the other side of both ropes, with your back to the ropes.

38   *Chinese Jump-Rope*

Star of David – Psalm 100

DIRECTIONS:

To make the star shape, you will need three people to hold two ropes of equal length. Make two triangles that overlap and point in opposite directions. Make sure the points are big enough to jump into. This game includes three basic moves. The moves are numbered and described below and then listed by number beside the line that accompanies the move.

1. Start in point 1, facing the middle. Jump into the middle, and at the same time, turn a half turn to face point 1. Jump into the opposite point—point 4— turning another half turn in the air to land facing away from the middle.

2. Step into the center, and face point 1. Then jump forward into that point and then backward into the center again.

3. Now, stand inside point 1. Jump to the next point, and jump all the way around the star without jumping into the middle.

■ **Shout for joy.** *(Perform move number 1, starting in point 1 and going to point 4.)*

■ **Worship the Lord.** *(Perform move number 1, starting in point 2 and going to point 5.)*

■ **Lord is God.** *(Perform move number 1, starting in point 3 and going to point 6.)*

■ **He made us.** *(Perform move number 2, into and out of point 1.)*

■ **We're his people.** *(Perform move number 2, into and out of point 2.)*

■ **Give him thanks.** *(Perform move number 2, into and out of point 3.)*

■ **God be praised.** *(Perform move number 2, into and out of point 4.)*

■ **The Lord's good.** *(Perform move number 2, into and out of point 5.)*

■ **His love's forever.** *(Perform move number 2, into and out of point 6.)*

■ **He is faithful.** *(Begin move number 3, into points 1, 2, and 3.)*

■ **To all generations.** *(Finish move number 3, into points 4, 5, and 6.)*

SCRIPTURE REFERENCE

▼

*Matthew
1:18-25;
Luke 1:26-45*

Angels, Angels

DIRECTIONS:

This game requires four children and two ropes—one rope longer than the other—to make the angel figure. Have two children stand with both feet inside one of the ropes, but twist it once between them to make an X. Have the other two children do the same but stand so their rope crosses the first rope. Have one of the children stand with legs farther apart to make the dress longer and wider at the bottom . During the game, make sure to have different children hold the ropes so that everyone has a chance to jump.

If you do not have enough children to hold the ropes, you may use chair or table legs. The jumpers will do ten moves to the rhyme. The moves are described by the word they are used with. The jumper will start in the dress, area 1.

■ Angels, angels, watching over me.
     1   2   3   4   5

1	2	3	4	5
Jump and land straddling the dress.	Jump and land in the wings with one foot in each wing.	Jump and turn around, landing with one foot in each wing again, but facing the other direction.	Jump and land in the dress.	Jump and land straddling the dress.

■ Angels, angels, stay with me.

6-a   6-b

6-a

Make a twistie. To do this, squeeze your ankles together with the ropes between them.

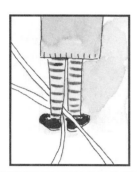

6-b

Jump to turn around still holding the ropes together, so you are facing the other direction. Jump up and allow the ropes to slip off feet and land inside the dress.

■ Angels, angels, all around.

7   8   9   10

7	**8**	**9**	**10**
Jump and land in the right wing.	Jump and land in the head.	Jump and land in the left wing.	Jump and land in the dress again, one jump per word.

■ Angels, angels, touch the ground.

11   12

11

Jump and land with feet on top of ropes where the wings cross the dress so that your feet are on three ropes.

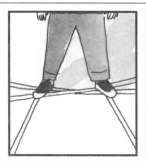

12

Jump off the ropes and land in the dress and touch the ground at the same time.

Cross

DIRECTIONS:

This game requires four players and two ropes—one rope longer than the other—to create the cross. The people holding the ropes will form the basic position with the two ropes crossing each other.

The other children will take turns being the jumper. The jumper will start by standing in the area labeled 2, facing area number 5. Kids will perform a series of eight actions to the rhyme. The moves are described beside their corresponding lines.

■ L-O-V-E

Jump and land straddling the nearest side rope of square 1, still facing square 5.

■ That is what Jesus gives to me.

Jump and land straddling the other side rope of square 1.

■ H-O-P-E

Jump and land with both feet in square 9.

■ When I'm worried, I'll believe.

Jump and land with right foot in square 7 and left foot in square 3.

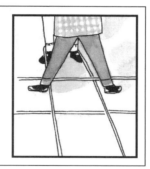

■ G-R-A-C-E

Jump and land with both feet on the two side ropes of square 5.

■ That is why Jesus died for me.

Jump and land straddling square 5.

■ J-O-Y

Make a twistie. To do this, squeeze ankles together, with ropes between. Turn around to face square 1.

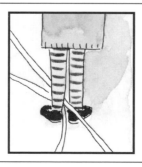

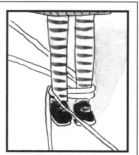

■ See it in my life.

Jump up and allow the ropes to slip off feet and land with both feet in square 5.

HAND GAMES

Psalm 47:1-2

"Clap your hands, all you nations,
Shout to God with cries of joy."

Hand-clapping games have been around for generations. Mothers often teach simple clapping games or finger games such as "Pat a Cake" or "The Itsy Bitsy Spider" to their young children. As children grow older, they make new rhymes and clapping combinations that are more interesting.

Hand-clapping games are played all over the world, from America to Africa to China. In Africa, China, Korea, and Japan, the children make up a combination of claps to a rhyme and repeat the combination faster and faster until it is impossible to continue. Another variation of hand-clapping games is Paper, Rock, Scissors. In Japan, the children sometimes use the names "Fox, Magistrate, Gun," and hold out different fingers rather than make a shape with their hands.

Hand-clapping can be done anytime and anywhere, since all kids need is four hands. Many children play hand-clapping games at recess time at school or at home with friends. One friend told us that her daughter and a friend play these games in the grocery store while she shops.

To use these rhymes, practice the moves before teaching the rhyme to the children. Then your children can clap away anywhere, at any time. Since these games are so easy to play anywhere, children in other places will hear them and want to learn them, spreading the message of God's love in a fun, new way.

Hand Clap Games Key:

1.
Clap hands together.

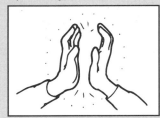

2.
Clap right hand to partner's right hand.

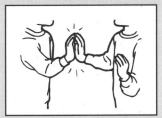

3.
Clap left hand to partner's left hand.

4.
Clap both hands to both of partner's hands.

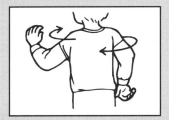

5.
Clap hands on thighs.

6.
Stomp feet.

7.
Roll hands, beginning at waist level.

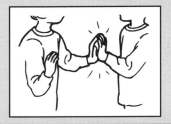

8.
Turn around.

9.
Cross arms and put hands on your shoulders.

10.
Cup both palms with hands together and pretend to scoop the air.

11.
Point to self.

12.
Point to partner.

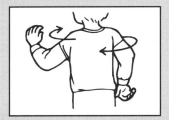

13.
Place your open right hand thumb up at about face level and clap your partners right hand in the same position.

14.
Make a circle with right hand and pretend to scoop the air.

15.
Make a circle with left hand and pretend to scoop the air.

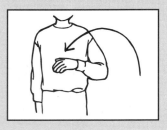

16.
Put right hand behind right ear, repeat with left hand and left ear.

17.
Shake right hands, then shake left hands.

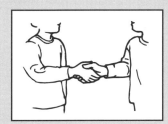

18.
Place open left hand with thumb up at about waist level and clap your partners left hand in the same position.

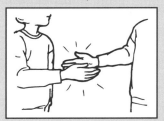

19.
Place hands palms together, as if praying. Both people move hands to the left so that the backs of the left hands clap together. Continue to slide hands to the left across partner's. Slide them back to the right so that the backs of the rights hands clap against partner's right hand, and then into beginning position.

20.
Move right hands out of the way and clap left hands. Leave left hands together.

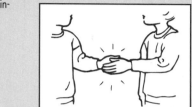

21.
Clap partner's right hand above the left hands.

22.
Move right hand down to clap your own hands together.

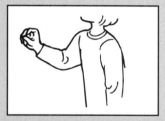

23.
With right hand grab partner's right hand below the left hands.

24.
With left hand grab partner's left hand below the right hands. Keep left hands together for the next three moves.

25.
With right hand, clap your own right thigh.

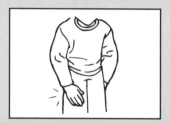

26.
Snap with right hand.

27.
At about face level, move right hand toward partner's right hand and clap the hands together. Continue to move hand to the left. Then go back to the right and clap the backs of right hands against each other.

28.
Both people hold arms out in front and cross them, so that right hands are clasped together, and left hands are clasped together. Swing arms back and forth.

29.
Put one hand at waist level, palm up. Put other hand palm down at shoulder height. Have partner do the opposite. Move hands in opposite directions so that they clap together. Turn hands over and do the same thing in the opposite direction.

30.
Snap with right hands, snap with left hands, then snap with both.

Joseph

DIRECTIONS:

Use the following series of moves for each line of this rhyme.

5	5	1	1	13	18	4	4

1. Jo-seph had a spe-cial co-at,
    A great coat of ma-ny co-lors.
    He went way out in-to the field,
    To find all his ma-ny bro-thers.

2. His bro-thers did not like him much,
    They put him down in-to a well.
    When some trav-el-ers came b-y,
    Poor bro-ther Jo-seph they did sell.

3. He was sold a-gain to Poti-phar,
    Who's wife brought Joseph much trouble.
    In-to jail they put poor Jo-seph
    Where he met king's ser-vants dou-ble.

4. But God gave Jo-seph quite a gift,
    By tell-ing him what the dreams meant.
    When Pha-raoh had a fright-ful dream,
    From jail to Pha-raoh Jo-seph went.

5. Then E-gypt stored up so much food,
    For sev-en won-der-ful ye-ars.
    So when the fa-mine came a-long,
    In E-gypt there were no more tears.

6. Jo-seph's bro-thers trav-eled fa-r,
    To get some food so they could eat.
    Un-til they came to E-gy-pt,
    Where bro-ther Jo-seph they did meet.

7. They did not rec-og-nize hi-m,
    The first ti-me that th-ey met.
    So Jo-seph did some th-ings,
    That real-ly cau-sed them to sweat.

8. But the bro-thers were re-li- eved,
    When bro-ther Jo-seph showed him-self.
    And his fa-ther was so hap-py,
    His boys a-gain num-bered twe-lve.

Down by the Banks of the Jordan River

SCRIPTURE REFERENCE

▼

Joshua 3-4

RHYME:

Down by the banks of the Jordan River

Where the Israelites crossed from bank to bank.

A singin', "God has made me free."

Splish splash with a big kersplash.

DIRECTIONS:

If there are more than two people, have everyone sit in a circle. Everyone puts both hands out to the side with right palms up and left palms down. Have everyone put a right hand on top of the left hand of the person next to him or her. The rhyme begins as one person uses his or her right hand to clap the right hand of the person to the left, who then claps the hand of the person to his or her left. The process continues around the circle until the rhyme is over. Do this as fast as you can. Whoever's hand is clapped at the last "splash" will start the next round of the game.

For two players, hold right hands, as if shaking hands, and push each other's hand back and forward. The child whose hand is back when you say "splash," has to sing the rhyme alone the next time.

David

Da-vid, Da-vid you're the best,

Un-afraid, not like the rest.

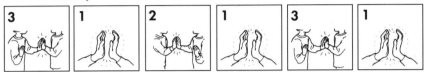

Go Da-vid. *(Snap fingers twice.)* Go Da-vid. *(Snap fingers twice.)*

Da-vid, Da-vid, it is known

You hit Go-liath with a stone.

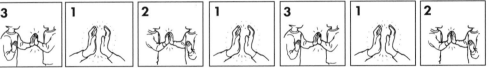

Go Da-vid. *(Snap fingers twice.)* Go Da-vid. *(Snap fingers twice.)*

Da-vid, Da-vid, you're so bright

You re-lied upon God's might

Go Da-vid. *(Snap fingers twice.)* Go Da-vid. *(Snap fingers twice.)*

Psalm 8

Our Lord, and our Ma-jes-ty

5 5 1 1 4 4 4

High-er than the earth and me.

5 5 1 1 6 6 6

Child-ren learn to give you praise.

5 5 1 1 4 4 4

We see your art ma-ny ways.

5 5 1 1 4 4 4

Moon and stars, you set in place,

5 5 1 1 4 4 4

Up a-bove the world, in space.

5 5 1 1 6 6 6

You care for us, al-ways true.

5 5 1 1 4 4 4

You made us low-er than you.

5 5 1 1 6 6 6

You give us glory, honor, and worth.

5 5 1 1 4 4 4

You put us in charge of the earth.

5 5 1 1 6 6 6

Stars, Stars

(Sing to the tune of "Twinkle, Twinkle, Little Star.")

Stars, stars, way up high,

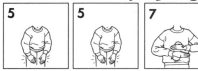

Up a-bove the big night sky.

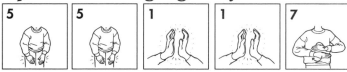

God made you, and God made me.

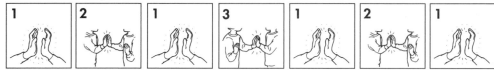

Loved us before we came to be.

Stars, stars, way up high,

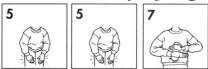

Up a-bove the big night sky.

I am growing big and strong,

Some-times don't know right from wrong.

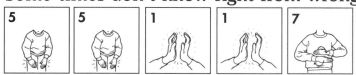

Seems like I am learn-ing slow,

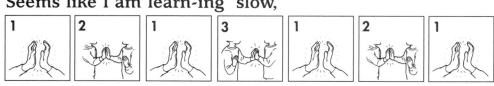

Ma-ny things I want to know.

I am growing big and strong,

Some-times don't know right from wrong.

God loves me and I love him,

So my light will never dim.

God has made my heart his home,

E-ven af-ter I am grown.

God loves me and I love him

So my light will never dim.

J-E-S-U-S

(Sing to the tune of "B-I-N-G-O.")

God sent his son to earth one day,

And Je-sus was his name, yeah.

J-E-S-U-S

J-E-S-U-S

J-E-S-U-S

And Je-sus was his name, yeah.

The Storm

SCRIPTURE REFERENCE

Matthew 8:23-27;
Mark 4:35-41;
Luke 8:22-25

(Sing to the tune of "A Sailor Went to Sea, Sea, Sea")
Use the following series of moves for each line of this rhyme.

The dis-ciples went to sea, sea, sea.

A storm came from the sea, sea, sea.

They woke Je-sus you see, see, see.

He calmed the great big sea, sea, sea.

He looked at them you see, see, see.

Said, "Where's your faith?" you see, see, see.

You need not fear the sea, sea, sea.

So trust the Lord, you see, see, see.

Peter Walks on Water

(Sing to the tune of "Miss Mary Mac.")
Use the following series of moves for each line of this rhyme.

9	5	1	2	1	3	1	2

A man named Pe-ter, Pe-ter, Pe-ter,

Did walk on wa-ter, wa-ter, wa-ter,

Out to see Je-sus, Je-sus, Je-sus.

As he walked out, out, out,

He looked a way, way, way,

From Jesus' eyes, eyes, eyes,

And he did fall, fall, fall.

And Peter said "Lord, Lord, Lord,

I'm gonna drown, drown, drown."

Then his friend Je-sus, Je-sus, Je-sus,

Did grab his hand, hand, hand,

Then they did walk, walk, walk,

Back to the boat, boat, boat,

Where Peter did stay, stay, stay,

The rest of the night, night, night.

Fruits of Galilee

This works well when teaching about life in Bible times and the foods that were eaten then.

Figs in a basket,

Dates in a bowl,

Olives on the table,

1, 2, 3,

Grown in Gal-i-lee.

All Together Friends

All together friends.

I love Je-sus!

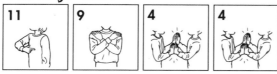

And he loves me!

No mat-ter what col-or I may be.

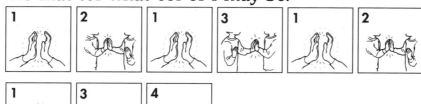

He loves us,   **He loves you!**

E-ven when you're feel-ing blue.

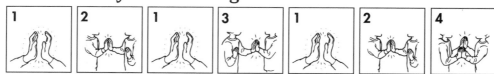

All together friends.

Itsy Bitsy Zacchaeus

SCRIPTURE REFERENCE

▼

Luke 19:1-9

(Sing to the tune of "The Itsy Bitsy Spider.")
This rhyme involves some sign language for some of the words, so you will want to spend some time practicing the motions before trying to teach this to your kids.

■ Itsy Bitsy Zacchaeus,
1   2   3

1	**2**	**3**
Put one hand out palm up and the other hand above it palm down.	Move them closer together until the end of the line.	At the end of the line, clap both hands to both of partner's hands twice.

■ Climbed up the sycamore tree,
4   5

4	**5**
Make the motion of climbing a tree, until the end of the line.	Have both children clap their own hands together, twice.

■ As he looked down, my Jesus he did see.
6   7   8   9   10

6	**7**	**8**	**9**	**10**
Make a circle with thumb and forefinger of both hands, put them up to eyes and look down.	Place hand on chest, palm flat.	Then touch the middle finger of your right hand to the open palm of the left hand, and touch the middle finger of the left hand to the palm of the right hand.	Next, make a V with the forefinger and middle finger of right hand, turn palm towards face, touch cheek below eyes with fingers, and move hand forward.	At the end of the line, have the children clap both their hands to both of their partner's hands.

■ Then Jesus said, "Won't you please come down to me?"
11   12   13   14   15

11	**12**	**13**	**14**	**15**
Touch the middle finger of your right hand to the open palm of the left hand, and touch the middle finger of the left hand to the palm of the right hand.	Hold up the forefinger of right hand, touch your chin, and then move hand forward.	Then put your hand on your chest and move it in circles.	Move hands up and away from your body and then bring them back, as if motioning someone to come down.	At the end of the line, have the children clap both their hands together.

■ Then Itsy Bitsy Zacchaeus was happy as could be.
16   17   18

16	**17**	**18**
Put one hand out palm up and the other hand above it palm down.	Move them closer together until the end of the line.	At the end of the line, have the children clap both their hands to both their partner's.

Lydia

Acts 16:11-15

Lydi-a, Lydi-a,

Lydi-a from Thy-a-ti-ra.

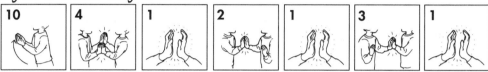

Sit-ting by a riv-er,

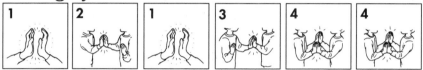

With her purple cloth,

Listening to Paul,

Teach, preach, teach, teach, ta-teach preach.

Teach, preach, teach, teach, ta-teach preach.

Listen, listen, o-o-wah, listen, listen.

Listen, listen, o-o-wah, listen, listen.

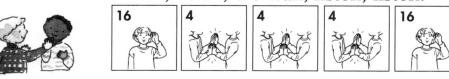

A, B, C, D, E, F, G,

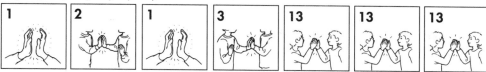

Lydi-a was saved by Paul you see.

She was bap-tized that day,

That is all I have to say.

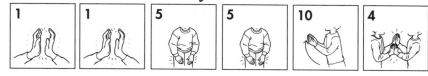

SCRIPTURE REFERENCE
▼

*Matthew
27:33–28:15;
Mark
15:21–16:20;
Luke
23:26–24:12;
John 3:16;
John
19:17–20:9;
1 John 1:9*

ABC

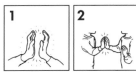

Use the following series of moves for each line of this rhyme.

A, B, C, D, E, F, G,

Je-sus loves me, e-ven me.

H, I, J, K, L, M, N, O, P

Jesus has come for both you and me.

Q, R, S, T, U, V,

On the cross he died you see.

W, X, Y, and Z,

Je-sus rose a-gain for me.

My Friend

(Sing to the tune of "Say, Say My Playmate.")

Say, say my Je-sus,

You came to die for me.

From sin to set me free,

You made a home for me,

Way up in hea-ven,

A place called paradise.

And I will love you for-ev-er more, more, more.

One, Two

Jeremiah 10:10;
John 17:3;
1 John 5:20

1, 2, God is true.

3, 4, God is more.

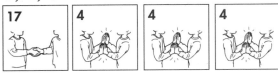

5, 6, God's love is rich.

7, 8, God is great.

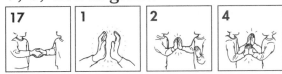

9, 10, God will win.

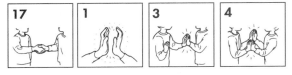

STRING GAMES

For generations, children around the world have loved games played with a loop of string wrapped around their fingers and held between their hands. (Some of our grandmothers even played Cat's Cradle under their desks at school.) With a simple string, children can make many shapes and play many types of games.

One of the most popular games, Cat's Cradle, is found all over the world and has various names. In India it is called Scissors, while *Umuzwa* (Wooden Spoon) is the name from the Ulungu of Tanganyika. To children in England, Australia, and the United States it's called String Puzzle, Picking Up and Taking Off, or just Taking Off. Although the North American Indians call this game Crow's Feet, in China it is called Sawing Wood. *Na-ash-klo*, or Continuous Weaving, is what the Navajos call it. Japanese children call this game *Aya-ito-tori* (Woof Pattern String Taking), and the people of Celebes call it *Toeka-Toeka*, (Ladder-Ladder).

TEACHER TIP
These moves are easy to do if you try them as you read the instructions. It is best to learn the moves well and then to learn the rhymes to say as you make the string figures.

Cat's Cradle is made up of a series of figures created when one player takes the string off another player's hands, and then grabs and pulls various combinations of strings. Even some of the different figures made during the game have names.

You can play these games anywhere as long as you have a string that is about sixty inches long. Try our games, and then see if you can come up with your own. Use these amazing "tricks" as tools to pass along and remember important Bible truths. Enjoy!

BASIC FOREFINGER POSITION

1. Hook string over your thumbs and pinkies of both hands, with the string on the palm side, inside of the other fingers.
2. With the forefinger of your right hand, pick up the string on your left hand between the thumb and pinkie.
3. With the forefinger on your left hand, do the same, but make sure you pick up the string inside the loop created in step 2.

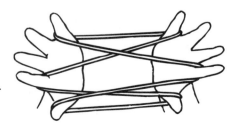

Crown

RHYME:

God is our great King.
That is why we sing.

DIRECTIONS:

1
Begin with the forefinger position.

2
With your thumbs, pick up the near forefinger string. Now you have two loops on your thumbs.

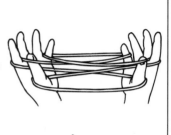

3
Take the bottom loop of the two, and move it up and over the thumb. You can do this with your mouth or with the thumb and forefinger of your opposite hand.

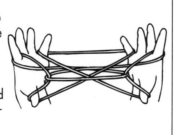

4
Drop your pinkie strings. Now you have an upside-down cup and saucer.

5
Where the cup and saucer "join" you will notice a triangle. With your pinkies, go over the nearest string and pick up the top string of this triangle. Pull your pinkies back to their original position.

6
You'll notice a string that goes straight across on the far side of your forefingers. Grab this with your teeth. Bring your head up, and tip your hand so that your thumbs are up. You have completed the pattern.

Tower of Babel

RHYME:

Building, building, big and tall,
Did not honor God at all.
God changed your language on that day.
Learn from them and God obey.

DIRECTIONS:

1
Begin with forefinger position.

2
With your thumbs, reach over the thumb string farthest from your body and the nearer forefinger string. Pick up the far forefinger string.

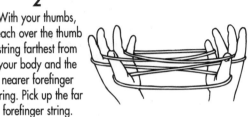

3
The thumbs should now have two loops. Carefully take the bottom loop up and over the thumbs. You may have to do this with your teeth.

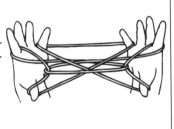

4
Drop the pinkie strings. Rotate your hands so that the cup and saucer are upright.

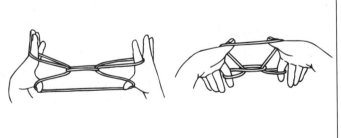

5
With your teeth, grab the top of the cup. Drop the loops on your thumbs and pull your hands down, gently and slowly.

Angels Climbing the Ladder

*Genesis
28:10-22*

RHYME:

Angels from heaven climbed down a ladder,
God gave Jacob a lesson that did matter.

DIRECTIONS:

1
Begin with forefinger position.

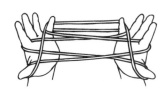

2
With your pinkie fingers, pick up the thumb string nearest your body and pull it back.

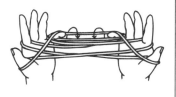

3
Your pinkie should have two loops on it now. By using your teeth or your thumb and forefinger of the opposite hand, take the bottom of the two loops up and over your pinkies.

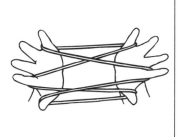 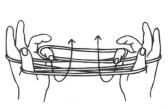

4
There is a string that goes across the inside of your forefingers. Bend your forefingers down, and hold it tight.

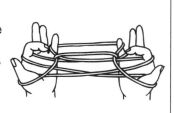

5
Twist your hands away from you. Without letting go of any of the strings, set the far pinkie string on the floor and put your foot on it.

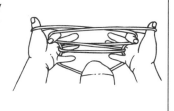

6
Hold tightly to the forefinger string. Now drop the pinkie and the thumb strings.

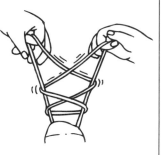

7
Now, slowly and gently, pull up with your right forefinger and then your left. Continue moving your hands until the angel gets to the top of the ladder.

Manger With Legs

RHYME:

In the manger Jesus did lay,
On a bed made of hay.

DIRECTIONS:

1
Loop string over the forefingers and ring fingers of both hands.

2
With the middle finger of your right hand, pick up the string that goes across the middle finger of your left hand.

3
Do the same with your left hand.

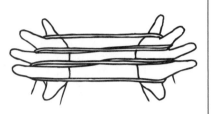

4
Each thumb will go under the strings. One thumb will hook over the second and third strings, and the other thumb will hook over the fourth and fifth strings. Pull the thumb strings down to create the legs of the manger.

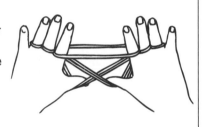

Butterfly

RHYME:

Butterfly in the sky,
Waving as you go by.
God made you, God made me.
That's how it's meant to be.

DIRECTIONS:

1
Begin with forefinger position.

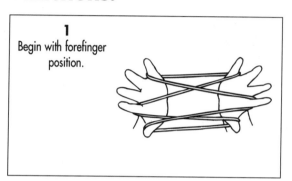

2
Move your thumbs over and underneath the forefinger strings farthest from your body. Pull them back. The thumbs should now have two loops.

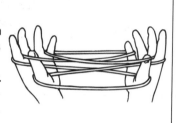

3
Of the two loops on the thumbs, take the bottom loop up and over the thumbs.

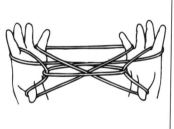

4
Drop the loops on your little fingers.

5
Stretch your hands out and your fingers down.

6
Move your thumb up into the loop on the forefinger. Now there should be two loops on your thumbs.

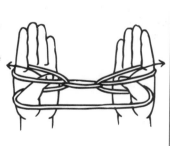

7 Of the two loops on the thumbs, take the bottom loop up and over the thumbs. 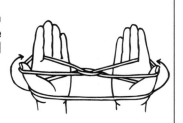	**8** You will see a string that goes straight across the other strings. Hook your forefinger over that string and down into the triangular shaped loop, between the thumb and forefinger. 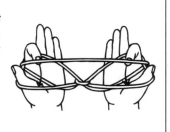

9 Turn your hands so that the backs face you, and stretch your fingers out to create the pattern.

Ark

SCRIPTURE REFERENCE

▼

Genesis 6–8

RHYME:

Here is Noah's big, big boat,
Do you think that it will float?

DIRECTIONS:

1
Do the first three steps of the manger. (See page 69.)

2
Put both thumbs under the strings, and then hook them over the second and third strings, and pull down.

3
Put your forefingers under the fourth and fifth strings. Keep these strings near the top of the fingers, and be careful not to lose the strings already at the bottom of these fingers. Pull your forefingers up, and you have Noah's ark.

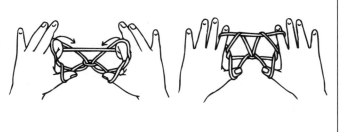

SCRIPTURE REFERENCE

▼

Matthew 1:18-25;
Luke 1:26-45

Angel

RHYME:

Angels, angels in the air,
God is the one who put them there.

DIRECTIONS:

(For this one, a smaller string shows the angel better.)

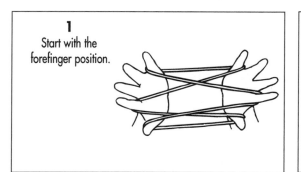

1
Start with the forefinger position.

2
With your thumbs, reach over all the strings and hook your thumbs under the farthest string. You will have two loops on your thumbs.

3
Using your mouth or the thumb and forefinger of your opposite hand, take the bottom string from each thumb and place it on the pinkies. Make sure you don't drop any of the other strings.

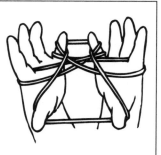

4a
For each hand, take the far string on the forefinger, and move it over onto the middle finger.

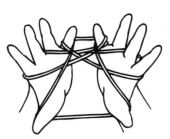

4b
The head of the angel is at the pinkies, wings are on the forefingers and middle fingers, and the bottom of the dress is between the thumbs.

Goblet

SCRIPTURE
REFERENCE
▼

*Matthew
26:17-30;
Mark 14:12-25;
Luke 22:7-20*

RHYME:

Jesus drank from this cup,
With the disciples he did sup.

DIRECTIONS:

1
Hook the string over the thumbs.

2
With your pinkies, pick up the thumb string nearest to you.

3
With the forefinger of the right hand, pick up the string that goes across your left hand.

4
With the forefinger of your left hand, pick up the string that goes across your right hand.

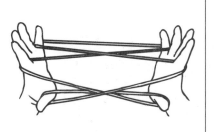

5
Drop thumb strings.

6
With your thumbs pick up the far pinkie strings.

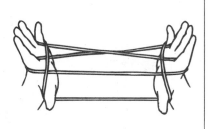

7
You now have a straight line that goes from your pinkies to your thumbs. With the middle finger of your right hand, pick up that string on your left hand.

8
Do the same with the middle finger of the left hand; make sure you pick up the string inside the loop created in step 7.

9
Turn your hands upward and toward your body until your fingers point toward you and your pinkies point up toward your face. Your palms should still be facing each other.

10
Squeeze together your forefinger, middle finger, ring finger, and pinkie on each hand. Stretch out your thumbs as far as possible.

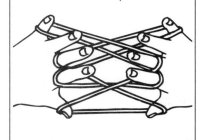

Fish

RHYME:

Little fish in the Sea of Galilee,
Into Peter's net, a miracle to see.

DIRECTIONS:

This string pattern will present more of a challenge for those kids who have mastered the easier patterns. Encourage your children by comparing this to the actual task of fishing—it takes a lot of time and practice, with the reward not coming for quite a while.

1
Begin with forefinger position.

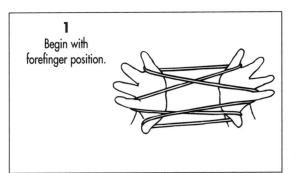

2
Drop the thumb strings.

3
Reach your thumbs under all of the strings, and hook your thumbs on the farthest pinky string, and pull it back under all the other strings.

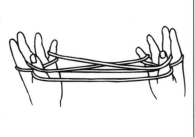

4
Without dropping the string that is already on your thumbs, move your thumbs over the second string and hook them under the third string. Pull this string back.

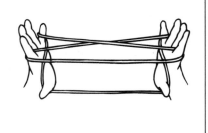

5
Drop the pinkie strings.

6
With the pinkies, go over the string that is nearest them and pick up the next string. Pull the pinkies back to their place along with this string.

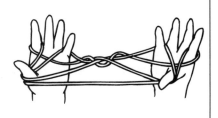

7

Drop both of the loops on the thumbs.

8

With your thumbs, reach across the first two strings and hook the third string. Pull these strings back toward you.

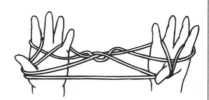

9

With your thumbs, pick up the string on each forefinger that is nearest the thumbs. It is important that you pick it up where it touches each forefinger. This loop should be on both the thumb and the forefinger.

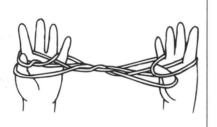

10

Take the bottom loops on the thumbs up and over the other loop, and over the thumb.

11

You will see a triangle formed between each thumb and forefinger. Put your forefingers down into the triangles and hold your forefingers fingers tightly against your hands.

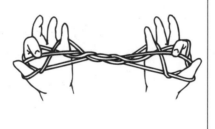

12

Drop the pinkie strings, and stretch out your thumbs and forefinger, with your palms facing out. This is a difficult step, so you may need to try it several times.

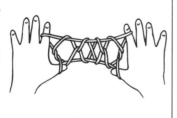

13

Carefully set down the left-hand side, so you don't change the shape. Put your left forefinger, middle finger, and ring finger inside the nearest diamond. Pick up the strings using these fingers, and stretch out your middle finger as far as possible to make the fish's head.

14

Take the loop on the thumb of right hand and loop it over the forefinger so both the thumb and forefinger are in the loop. Take the loop on the forefinger, and loop it over the thumb. Now you should have both loops around both fingers. This will be the tail.

15

To make the body, squeeze the remaining three diamonds as close together as possible and as close to the tail as possible. Now you have a fish.

Star of David

RHYME:

Six points all around,
God kept David safe and sound.

DIRECTIONS:

(The Star of David requires two people.)

1

The first person will wrap the string once around both wrists, making one loop completely around the wrists. With the middle finger of the right hand, pick up the string where it goes across the inside of your wrist. Do the same with your left middle finger, inside the loop just created.

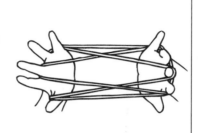

2

The second person grabs the X's on each side of the figure with his or her thumb and forefinger. Pinch the X's, and pull these strings out past the side strings, and then go under the side strings and come up inside the middle. Take the string off the first person's hands. Spread your hands and fingers apart.

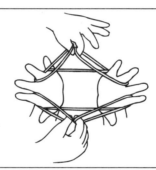

3

With the forefinger and thumb of each hand, the first person grabs the two X's in the middle.

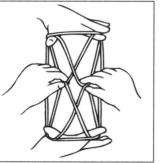

4

Pull your fingers out and over the side strings as far as possible. This creates a star pattern.

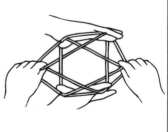

BALL GAMES

G o to any playground, and you'll see children bouncing balls or playing dodge ball, four square, kickball, or football. Kids play with baseballs, footballs, golf balls, and rubber bouncy balls—big and small. The materials balls are made from also have great variety—from rubber to leather to plastic. Even lemons and limes have been used as balls!

The first ball might have been a rock or an animal skull. As time passed, children and adults began to use wood, cork, or leather stuffed with various items to make a ball shape. Native Indians used balls made of wrapped strips of bark covered with the gum and sap of trees to hold them together. Some wove grasses or weeds to make balls. Around 1839, rubber balls came out on the market, and children began to play bouncy ball games.

There are all kinds of ball games. Some have been played for a long time, and others are relatively new. Soccer (called football in Europe) and rugby are older games, while dodge ball, four square, and kickball are more modern.

Some of the games in this book are based on familiar children's ball games, whereas others are new. All can be used to review and remember important Bible lessons.

Books of the Bible

DIRECTIONS:

Any number of players may play this game. Have children form groups of four or five. Each team must have a bouncy ball, such as a basketball. Recite the books of the New Testament to the tune of "Ten Little Indians." As you recite, one child will bounce the ball a certain way for each group of books. That child will then pass the ball to the next child for the next stanza of the song.

Genesis, Exodus, Leviticus, Numbers, *(Bounce the ball in front of you.)*
Deuteronomy, Joshua, Judges, Ruth, *(Bounce the ball under your left leg.)*
1 Samuel, 2 Samuel, 1 and 2 Kings, *(Bounce the ball in front of you.)*
1 and 2 Chronicles, *(Bounce the ball under your right leg.)*
(Bounce ball to the next player.)

Ezra, Nehemiah, Esther, Job, *(Bounce the ball in front of you.)*
Psalms, Proverbs, Ecclesiastes, *(Bounce the ball under your left leg.)*
Song of Solomon, Isaiah, Jeremiah, *(Bounce the ball in front of you.)*
Then comes Lamentations, *(Bounce the ball under your right leg.)*
(Bounce ball to the next player.)

Ezekiel, Daniel, Hosea, Joel, *(Bounce the ball in front of you.)*
Amos, Obadiah, Jonah, Micah, *(Bounce the ball under your left leg.)*
Nahum, Habakkuk, Zephaniah, *(Bounce the ball in front of you.)*
Haggai, Zechariah, and Malachi *(Bounce the ball under your right leg.)*
(Bounce ball to the next player.)

Matthew, Mark, Luke, and John, *(Bounce the ball in front of you.)*
Acts, Romans, 1 and 2 Corinthians, *(Bounce the ball under your left leg.)*
Galatians, Ephesians, Philippians, Colossians, *(Bounce the ball in front of you.)*
1 and 2 Thessalonians, *(Bounce the ball under your right leg.)*
(Bounce ball to the next player.)

1 and 2 Timothy, Titus, *(Bounce the ball in front of you.)*
Philemon, Hebrews, James, 1st and 2nd and Peter, *(Bounce the ball under your left leg.)*
1st John, 2nd John, and 3rd John, *(Bounce the ball in front of you.)*
Jude, and Revelation. *(Bounce the ball under your right leg.)*

Creation Ball

DIRECTIONS:

Have children form two groups to play this game. If you have mixed age levels, be sure to group younger children with older children. The players will need either chalk or tape, to mark off the boxes on the ground, and a bouncy ball, such as a four-square ball. The object of this game is to have the ball land in the boxes representing all seven days of creation, in order, as children say what was created each day. To set up the game, mark out eight boxes on the ground or floor next to a wall, and number them as shown in the illustration. The first player stands in the first box and tosses the ball against the wall, trying to make it bounce into the box labeled Day 1. If the ball bounces in the appropriate square, the player must say what God created on that day. The player then tries to bounce the ball off the wall and into the next box. If the player fails to get the ball into the correct box, then the next player on the other team takes a turn. At the end of seven tries, each team can take a rest!

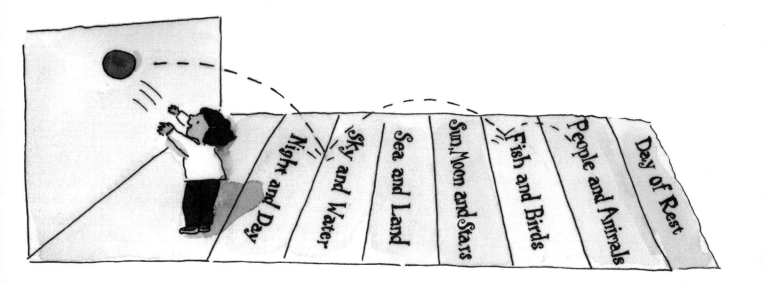

Ball Commandments

DIRECTIONS:

You can play Ball Commandments with any number of players, and the game is best played outside. All you need for this game is a bouncy ball, such as a four-square ball. The object of this game is to complete a certain movement for each of the Ten Commandments while the ball is in the air. Have children take turns throwing the ball as high into the air as they can and completing the movements. When a child finishes one of the commandments, he or she may then continue on to the next commandment. If the child fails to catch the ball or makes a mistake, the child will then pass the ball to another child.

COMMANDMENT ONE

SAY: **You will be my only God**. *(Throw the ball into the air. Then catch the ball before it bounces.)*

COMMANDMENT TWO

SAY: **I will not make any idols.** *(Throw the ball into the air. Jump and cross your legs in the air. Land with legs crossed. Jump to uncross your legs. Catch the ball before it bounces.)*

COMMANDMENT THREE

SAY: **I will respect the name of the Lord my God.** *(Throw the ball into the air. Hop on one leg, then hop on the other, and then hop on the first leg again. Then catch the ball.)*

COMMANDMENT FOUR

SAY: **I will keep the Sabbath day holy.** *(Throw the ball into the air. Clap your hands twice in front of you and then twice behind your back. Then catch the ball.)*

COMMANDMENT FIVE

SAY: **I will obey my mom and dad.** *(Throw the ball into the air. Twirl around once. Then catch the ball.)*

COMMANDMENT SIX

SAY: **I will not kill anyone.** *(Throw the ball into the air. Do a jumping jack. Then catch the ball.)*

COMMANDMENT SEVEN

SAY: **I will stay faithful to whomever I marry.** *(Throw the ball into the air. Clap your hands above your head, in front of you, behind your back, and in front of you once more. Then catch the ball.)*

COMMANDMENT EIGHT

SAY: **I will not steal.** *(Throw the ball into the air. Touch the ground. Then catch the ball.)*

COMMANDMENT NINE

SAY: **I will not lie.** *(Throw the ball into the air. Jump and turn around while in the air. Then catch the ball.)*

COMMANDMENT TEN

SAY: **I will not want what others have.** *(Throw the ball into the air. Sit down and then catch the ball while sitting down.)*

Star Ball

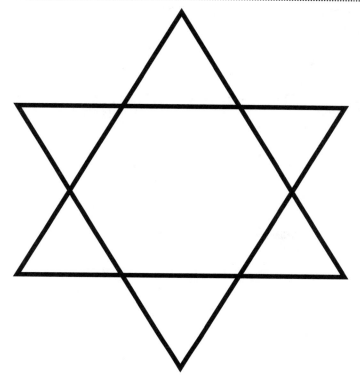

DIRECTIONS:

This game uses elements from the story of the feast at the palace of Belteshazzar and is similar to four square. It requires six or more players. Begin by drawing a large six-sided star on the ground. (You may do this by first drawing a large triangle and then drawing an upside-down triangle of the same size on top of the first one.) Decide which point is number 1, and then continue to number the others (2 through 6) clockwise around the star. The points could also be named after David and five of his children. Have a child stand inside each point. The person in point 1 will be the server. This person begins the game. The server must first bounce the ball one time in his or her own area and then must pass the ball to any of the other five players. To make a pass, the ball must bounce in the center of the star, then go to the receiver's point.

The server is out if the receiver catches the ball before it bounces in his or her area, if the ball misses the receiver's point, or if the ball bounces on a line. The receiver must catch the ball after one bounce in his or her area. If the server succeeds in bouncing the ball in the receiver's point and the receiver does not catch the ball, the receiver is out. The players must stay inside their points. If they step out for any reason other than to get a stray ball, they will be out.

When a person is out, the players in the lower areas will all rotate up one point. If you have more than six players, have the extra players form a line near point 6. The first player in line will move into point 6, and the player who was out will go to the end of the line. If you have only six players, the player who is out will go to point 6.

continued

The moves described below may be used in the game. (Before a player uses any of these moves, the player must call out the name of the move he or she wishes to make so the other players know what is happening.)

Flaming arrow—Bounce the ball as hard as possible so that it bounces really high and may go right over the receiver's head. Flaming arrows were used in the wars fought during the reign of Belteshazzar.

Palace Feast—To begin this, one player must call Palace Feast and at the same time call out the name of the player he or she wishes to have the Palace Feast with. The two players throw the ball back and forth to each other and not to any other players. When the players are tired of this move, one of them must call out, "Handwriting on the Wall." Belteshazzar was having a great feast in his palace at the time the handwriting appeared on the wall.

Handwriting on the Wall—One of the two players playing the Palace Feast calls out this name. The player with the ball may now throw it to whoever they wish. A feast at the palace of Belteshazzar, Nebuchadnezzar's son, was stopped when a hand began writing a message from God on the wall. The people were so frightened to see a hand, without a body, writing on the wall that they all ran away.

Grace

DIRECTIONS:

A basketball and a basketball hoop are needed for this game, which any number of children may play. Be sure the hoop is at a height appropriate for the age group playing the game. To begin, pick a Bible word from the list below. Have the players line up single file behind the free-throw line, facing the hoop. Each player then takes a turn trying to make a basket. Each time a player takes a turn, he or she may make only one shot. If the player misses the basket, he or she is assigned the first letter of the chosen word. If the player succeeds in getting a basket, nothing is assigned to him or her. After the player has finished, he or she will go to the end of the line. When a person has finished the word, begin again with a new word. Some Bible words are suggested below, although any four- or five-letter word will work for this game. Remind children that this game is called Grace, because God shows us grace whenever we fail or sin.

Jesus, Bible, Glory, Prayer, Praise, Grace, Light

Lighthouse Hop

DIRECTIONS:

This game is a reminder that the Bible provides the light of truth for our lives. Any number of children may play this game, which is based on Follow the Leader. You will need chalk to draw the lighthouse, a bouncy ball, and a stone or marker for each child. Draw a lighthouse on the ground similar to the illustration. Write the name of a Bible-related category in each of the different areas of the lighthouse. The first child will hop into the first square and will do some sort of action with the ball while naming something from the category of that square. He or she will then throw the ball to the next child in line and will go to the end of the line. The next child must hop into the box and repeat whatever action the first child did while naming something different from that category. Each child in line will get a turn to jump into that square and repeat the actions of the first child while naming something new from that category. Repeat with a different child as the leader for each of the boxes on the pattern.

These are some suggested categories: Ten Commandments, twelve apostles, men in the Bible, women in the Bible, children in the Bible, Jesus' parables, Jesus' miracles, New Testament stories, Old Testament stories, fruit of the spirit, Beatitudes.

Character Ball

Character Ball (a variation of dodge ball) is best played with a large group—the larger the group, the more fun! You'll need only a bouncy ball and something to mark out the playing area, such as chalk. Draw two large boxes on the ground, one for each team, big enough to fit around all the players from each side, about six feet apart. Then split the group up into two equal teams. Have team members spread out in their box. Players should then pick a character from the Bible, without revealing whom they have chosen. It does not matter if two or more people choose the same character. One child on one team will begin the game by throwing the ball at a child on the other team. *It is important for all the children to understand they must not hit anyone above the waist. If someone hits a person above the waist, the person that threw the ball must go over to the other team.* If a player succeeds in hitting a player from the other team below the waist, the player who threw the ball must say, "Who are you? Please give me a clue." If after hearing the clue, the player guesses the character, then the hit player joins the other team and picks a new character to be. If the player cannot guess the character, play resumes with the other team getting the ball. If a child steps out of the box, the child must go over to the other team. The game ends when all the players are in the same box.

SCRIPTURE
REFERENCE
▼

Acts 13–28

Paul's Journeys

DIRECTIONS:

This game (based on the game kickball) is best played with eight or more players forming two teams. Set up a playing area similar to a baseball diamond. Each base will represent a place from one of Paul's missionary journeys. First base is Philippi, second is Thessalonica, third is Corinth, and home is Jerusalem. The team in the field will have one player to pitch; one player on each city; and if there are enough children, players in the outfield and a player behind Jerusalem to catch. The team members who kick will all be "Pauls." To play, the pitcher rolls the ball to the kicker, and the kicker kicks the ball. If the ball is caught before it bounces, then the player is out, or in jail. (Kids in jail may sing songs like Paul and Silas did!) If the kick is not caught, then the kicker runs to Philippi. If someone gets the ball and throws it to the first base keeper before the kicker gets there, the kicker goes to jail. The kicker may also be put in jail if someone throws the ball and tags him or her below the waist. As other players take their turns, the previous kickers attempt to go to the other cities (or bases) and back to Jerusalem. If a player fails to touch a base, he or she goes to jail. After three people go to jail, the other team gets a turn at the plate. Players may decide how long the game should last.

Leaving Egypt

SCRIPTURE
REFERENCE
▼

*Exodus
12:31-42;
13:17–14:31;
16:1–17:7;
20:1-21;
Joshua 3–4*

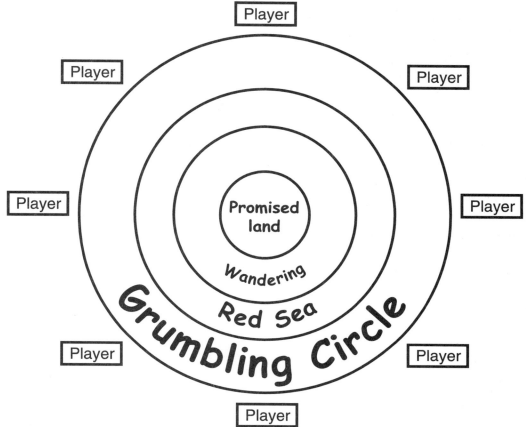

DIRECTIONS:

For this game, you will need a bouncy ball and chalk to draw out the playing area. The object of this game is to hit the ball into the circles labeled "Promised Land" or "Red Sea" and to avoid the circles labeled "Grumbling Circle" or "Wandering in the Wilderness." Before beginning, spend time with your group discussing the travels of the Israelites after they left Egypt, and be sure kids understand the connection between the Israelites experiences and the circles used in this game. To begin, draw concentric circles on the ground, starting with a circle twelve inches in diameter, then draw another circle eighteen inches out from the first one, a third circle out ten inches from the second, and the fourth circle out twenty-four inches from the third. Label these circles "Promised Land," "Wandering in the Wilderness," "Red Sea," and "Grumbling Circle." (See the illustration.) Players will stand around the circle, about three to five feet apart, depending on the number of children playing. Younger children may stand three to five feet away from the outer circle, and older children should stand five to ten feet away. Before play begins, choose a determined number of points to be reached. Assign a point value to each circle, with the inner circle having the highest value, the third circle having the next highest value, and the other two circles having negative values. The player must bounce the ball in front of him or her and then hit the ball toward the circles. If the ball bounces more than once in the playing area, the score is taken from the area where the ball first bounced. Play goes clockwise around the circle. The players continue playing the game until all of the players have reached the determined number of points.

Sowing Seeds

DIRECTIONS:

To play, you need yellow or green tennis balls, which will be the seeds; a baseball bat; and a large outdoor playing area. Mark off the playing area in twenty-foot increments. The pitcher will stand at the first twenty-foot mark. The area behind him to the next twenty-foot mark will be treated as the "Path," for one point; the twenty feet beyond that is the "Rocky Soil," for two points; the next twenty feet is the "Weeds," for three points; and anything beyond eighty feet is considered to be in "Good Soil," for four points. The pitcher will throw the ball to the batter, who tries to hit it to the "Good Soil" to get four points, which is called getting "A Good Crop." The hitter will try five times to hit the ball. The hitter will add up the points each time the ball lands, and any time he or she gets four points, the hitter gets "A Good Crop." After five attempts, the players switch. Be sure to discuss with your children how this game is like sowing the seeds of God's message of salvation, and that we all need to sow the seeds of the good news whenever we can. Other children may play as outfielders or catcher. Children take turns hitting. *Be sure the children know not to swing the bat when other children are too close.*

HOPSCOTCH GAMES

Hopscotch can be played with any number of players. The object of hopscotch is to throw a marker to different squares on a design and then to hop up the picture and back without falling over or stepping on a line. All you need for hopscotch is a piece of chalk, markers, and a playing area on which to draw the pattern. Draw the hopscotch pattern on the ground, making sure the drawing is large enough to jump in. From the box marked "start" (or right in front of the first box), the first player will throw the marker into the first box. That player must then hop over the box with the marker in it and land in box two. Continue to hop to the top of the pattern, landing in all the other squares, one at a time. If there are two boxes next to each other, the player may land with one foot in each box. When the player reaches the top of the design, he or she must turn around and hop back down the pattern. As the player hops back down, he or she must stop in the square before the square with the marker, pick up the marker, and then continue, being sure to hop in the square where the marker was.

Each player will take a turn throwing his or her marker. If a player succeeds at hopping up and back without any mistakes, the player will continue by throwing the marker into the next square. If a player makes a mistake, then he or she has to start over on the same square. It is considered a mistake if the marker lands in the wrong square or on a line, if the player lands on a line when jumping, if the player loses his or her balance and puts his or her other foot down when it is not appropriate, or if he or she steps in the square containing the marker.

Fish

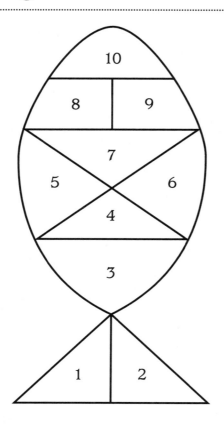

During creation, God made things in a special order. This way everything was ready for his best creation—people. People had a place to live, air to breath, food to eat, water to drink, and night for sleep. God even had a job for people, taking care of the plants and animals in the garden. This included the fishes in the sea. Use this fish to have fun.

Draw the fish pattern on the ground. Make sure the drawing is large enough to jump in. Play the game following the rules for hopscotch as explained in the introduction on page 87, but have children each tell one thing they can care for each time they toss their markers.

Adam's Tree

In the Garden of Eden there was a tree called the "tree of knowledge of good and evil." This is the tree that Adam and Eve ate from before they were banished from the Garden of Eden. The pattern for this hopscotch represents this tree. Be careful not to make a wrong step! Be sure to remind your children of the difference between willful sinning, as Adam and Eve did in their choices, and simply making mistakes, as kids might in this game.

Draw the tree pattern on the ground. Make sure the drawing is large enough to jump in. Play the game following the rules for hopscotch as explained in the introduction on page 87.

Butterfly

God created all sorts of animals—some of them beautiful like the butterfly. This hopscotch game focuses on the beauty of teamwork as two people work as a team to hop around the pattern.

Draw the butterfly pattern on the ground, making sure the drawing is large enough to jump in. Have children each find a partner to jump with. Have the two players hold on to each other, with one child in front of the other and the second child holding on to the first one's waist. Have one of the two children throw the marker into the first square and begin to hop along the pattern. The two players count as one person, so if one of the two lands on a line or puts a foot down, they both lose their turn and the next team tries. If a team succeeds in hopping up and back without any mistakes, the team continues to the next square. If a team makes a mistake, they have to start over on the same square.

Jacob's Ladder

Jacob had a dream in which he saw a ladder from heaven to earth. Angels used the ladder to travel between heaven and earth. See if you can travel safely up and down this ladder.

Draw the ladder pattern on the ground, making sure the drawing is large enough to jump in. Play the game following the rules for hopscotch explained in the introduction on page 87.

Ark

SCRIPTURE REFERENCE

▼

Genesis 6–9:17

When God flooded the earth and Noah was floating on the water with the animals, he probably had a lot of time with nothing to do! Maybe he and his family played games, like hopscotch. Even if they didn't, you can play this hopscotch game and you can think of the animals they had on the ark.

First, draw the ark pattern on the ground. Make sure the drawing is large enough to jump in. Play the game following the rules for hopscotch explained in the introduction on page 87, except that each time a child throws his or her marker, that child must name an animal that would have been on the ark.

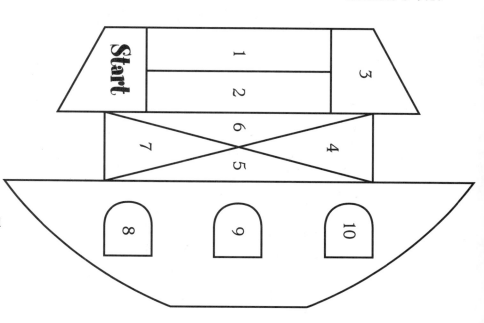

Rainbow

SCRIPTURE REFERENCE

▼

Genesis 9:1-17

After the flood, God put a rainbow in the sky to remind us that he will never again flood the entire earth. When some people see a rainbow, they like to say a pot of gold sits at the end of the rainbow. The real pot of gold is the special care that God takes of each of us, and the rainbow is a reminder of his love and care for each of us.

Draw the hopscotch rainbow pattern on the ground, making sure the drawing is large enough to jump in. Stand in the first cloud to throw the stone. Play the game following the hopscotch rules as described in the introduction on page 87, except that when children reach the other cloud, they should each name something they are thankful for.

Sailboat

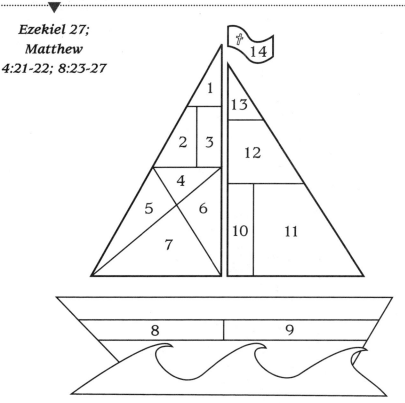

Even in the Old Testament times, people used boats to catch fish to eat and to travel across water. In the New Testament, Jesus often was involved with boats—calling disciples from working on boats, riding in boats, and even preaching from boats. Jump on this boat and try it out.

To begin with, draw the sailboat pattern on the ground. Make sure the drawing is large enough to jump in. Play the game following the hopscotch rules explained in the introduction on page 87, except have each child tell either a story about Jesus and a boat, or name one of the parables he taught from the boat.

Cross

*Matthew
27:33–28:15;
Mark
15:21–16:20;
Luke
23:26–24:12;
John 19:17–20:9*

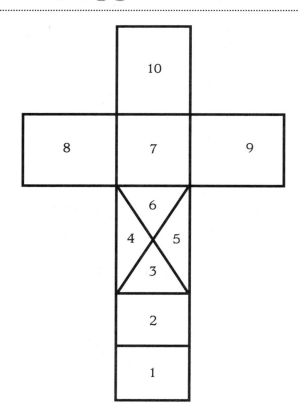

The cross is one of the most special symbols of Jesus we have. The cross shows us how much Jesus loved us—he was willing to die on a cross for us. However, Jesus didn't stay dead, and that's why the cross is empty. As you jump on this cross, remember how much Jesus loved you.

Before playing, draw the cross pattern on the ground, making sure the drawing is large enough to jump in. Play the game following the hopscotch rules as explained in the introduction on page 87, except that each time children throw their markers, they should name someone else who Jesus loves.

Fruit of the Spirit

The fruit of the spirit is a way to describe the good qualities that Jesus wants in each of our lives. The apple in this pattern represents love, because it is shaped like a heart.

The banana is for joy, because when it is held right, it looks like a big happy smile.

The pear is to show peace. Jesus wants to give us peace in our lives.

The orange represents patience. Patience is required to peel an orange to get to the sweet fruit inside!

The watermelon has seeds, and the seeds are like seeds of kindness that are spread around and will grow into bigger fruit.

The grapes symbolize goodness, because of the good things that come from grapes, like grape juice, jelly, and raisins. Grapes are even good just as they are!

Strawberry plants that produce strawberries all year long are called "ever-bearing" strawberries. The strawberries represent faithfulness. Jesus wants us to be faithful all the time.

The peach is for gentleness. Peaches are a soft and delicate fruit, and we should be careful to treat others as we would a peach.

The last fruit is self-control. When you eat cherries, you should use self-control or you may have a stomach ache! Jesus wants us to have self-control in all things we do.

Draw the fruit pattern on the ground. Make sure the drawing is large enough to jump in. Play this game following the hopscotch rules as described in the introduction on page 87. In addition, when children throw their markers into the squares, before jumping, they each must tell one way they can demonstrate that particular fruit, for example, "I can show kindness by being nice to my little sister."

Circle of Friends

When we believe in Jesus, we become part of God's special family. This hopscotch pattern shows us how God's family grows when more and more people believe in Jesus.

Draw the hopscotch pattern on the ground. Make sure the drawing is large enough to jump in. Follow the hopscotch rules as explained in the introduction on page 87, except that each time children throw their markers, they should each say the name of someone they want to tell about Jesus.

INDEXES